ANARCHY & INSURRECTION

ALFREDO BONANNO

FIRST DETRITUS BOOKS EDITION, 2022

Published in the USA by Detritus Books

DETRITUS BOOKS
OLYMPIA, WA
detritusbooks.com

Distributed by AK Press

Detritus Books ISBN: 978-1948501231

Printed in Canada

THE ANARCHIST TENSION

I AM ALWAYS SOMEWHAT EMBARRASSED WHEN I BEGIN A TALK, at least to start with. And this embarrassment increases in the case of what we mistakenly call conferences, or as one more modestly tries to camouflage them, conference-debates. After all, it is a question of someone turning up from elsewhere, perhaps from another generation, as though they have rained in from the past. Someone who stands in this classroom to give a talk and strangely, even dangerously, resembles those who hammer your brains with quite different intentions. If you listen carefully however you will find that, beyond appearances, there is a considerable difference in the concepts I am about to outline.

The first of these concepts takes the form of a question: What is anarchism? It might seem strange that I should take up such a problem in this situation as I know for certain that there are many anarchists here, because I know them personally. And if nothing else, anarchists should at least know what anarchism is. Yet it is necessary to take up the question "What is anarchism?" time and time again. Even in a few words. Why is that? This does not normally happen in other expressions of life, in other activities or ideas that define themselves with some foundation to be something or other.

So anarchists keep asking themselves the same question: What is anarchism? What does it mean to be an anarchist? Why? Because it is not a definition that can be made once and for all, put in a safe and considered a heritage to be tapped little by little. Being an anarchist does not mean one has reached a conclusion or said once and for all, "There, from now on I hold the truth and as such, at least from the point of view of the idea, I am a privileged person." Anyone who thinks like this is an anarchist in word alone. Instead the anarchist is someone who really puts themselves in doubt as such, as a person, and asks themselves: What is my life according to what I do and in relation to what I think? What connection do I manage to make each day in everything I do, a way of being an anarchist continually and not come to agreements, make little daily compromises, etc? Anarchism is not a concept that can be locked up in a word like a gravestone. It is not a political theory. It is a way of conceiving life, and life, young or old as we may be, whether we are old people or children, is not something final: it is a stake we must play day after day. When we wake up in the morning and put our feet on the ground we must have a good reason for getting up, if we don't it makes no difference whether we are anarchists or not. We might as well stay in bed and sleep. And to have a good reason we must know what we want to do because for anarchism, for the anarchist, there is no difference between what we do and what we think, but there is a continual transformation of theory into action and action into theory. That is what makes the anarchist unlike someone who has another concept of life and crystallizes this concept in a political practice, in political theory.

This is what is not normally said to you, this is what you never read in the newspapers, this is what is not written in books, this is what school jealously keeps quiet about, because this is the secret of life: never ever separate thought from action, the things we know, the things we understand, from the things we do, the things with which we carry out our actions.

Here is what distinguishes a politician from an anarchist revolutionary. Not the words, not the concepts and, allow me, in certain aspects not even the actions because it is not their extreme—let us say radical—conclusion in attack that differentiates and characterizes actions. It is not even accuracy in the choice of objective that qualifies them but it is the way in which the person, the comrade who carries out these actions, succeeds in making them become an expressive moment of their lives, a specific characterization, meaning, quality of life, joy, desire, beauty, not the practical achievement, not the sullen achievement of a deed that is mortally an end in itself and enables one to say; "I have done something today" far from myself, at the periphery of my existence.

There, that is one difference. And from this difference another emerges, a considerable one in my opinion. Anyone who thinks that things to be done are outside ourselves and are accomplished as a number of successes and failures—life is a staircase, at times you go up, at times you go down. There are times when things go well, and times when they go badly. There, whoever thinks life is made up of such things: for example, the classic figure of the democratic politician (for goodness' sake, someone you can talk to, a friendly guy, tolerant, who has a permissive side to him, believes in progress, in the future, in a better society, in freedom) well, a person like this, probably not wearing a double-breasted jacket, no tie, so casual, a person who close up looks like a comrade and who himself declares he is a comrade, this person could very well be a cop, it makes no difference. Why not? There are democratic policemen, the era of uniform repression is over, repression has friendly aspects today, they repress us with lots of brilliant ideas. How can we identify this person then, this democrat, how can we recognise him? And if he pulls the wool over our eyes to prevent us from seeing him, how can we defend ourselves from him? We can identify him through this fact: that for him life is production, his life is made up of doing things, a quantitative doing that unfolds before his eyes, and nothing else.

When we talk to someone we cannot ask to see their membership card. Their ideas often make us end up totally confused and unable to understand anything because we are all nice, progressive chatterboxes and all praise the beauty of tolerance and such like. How can we see that we have an enemy before us, the worst of our enemies? Because at least we could defend ourselves from the old fascist. He hit out, and if we were capable of it we hit him back, harder. Now things have changed, the situation has changed. It can even be difficult to fish out a fascist thug today. But the individual we are trying to describe, this democrat that we find all over the place, in school, Parliament, in the streets, or in the policeman's uniform, a judge, or a doctor, this fellow here is our enemy because he considers life in a different way to the way we consider it, because for him life is another kind of life, is not our life, because for him we are aliens and I don't see why we should consider him to be an inhabitant of our planet either. This is the dividing line between us. Because his concept of life is of a quantitative nature, because he measures things like success or, if you like, failure, but always from the quantitative point of view and we measure them differently and that is what we should be thinking about: in what way does life have a different meaning for us, a meaning that is qualitatively different?

So, this amiable gentleman wreaks criticism upon us and says, "Yes, anarchists are good people but they are ineffectual. What have they ever done in history? What State has ever been anarchist? Have they ever achieved government without a government? Isn't a free society, an anarchist society, a society without power, a contradiction?" And this critical rock that crashes down on us is certainly consistent, because in fact if you look closely at anywhere that anarchists got near to achieving their utopia of a free society such as in Spain or Russia, if you look at them closely, you find these constructions are somewhat open to criticism. They are certainly revolutions, but they are not libertarian revolutions, they are not *anarchy*.

So, when these gentlemen say, "You are utopians, you anarchists are dreamers, your utopia would never work," we must reply, "Yes, it's true, anarchism is a tension, not an end point, not a concrete attempt to bring about anarchy tomorrow morning." But we must also be able to say but you, distinguished democratic gentlemen in government that regulate our lives, that think you can get into our heads, our brains, that govern us through the opinions that you form daily in your newspapers, in the universities, schools, etc., what have you gentlemen accomplished? A world worth living in? Or a world of death, a world in which life is a flat affair, devoid of any quality, without any meaning to it? A world where one reaches a certain age, is about to get one's pension, and asks oneself, "But what have I done with my life? What has been the sense of living all these years?"

That's what you have accomplished, that is what your democracy is, your idea of the people. You are governing a people, but what does people mean? Who are the people? Are they perhaps that small, not even very significant, part who vote, go to the elections, vote for you, nominate a minority which in turn nominates another minority even smaller than the first that governs us in the name of the law? But what are these laws if not the expression of the interests of a small minority specifically aimed in the first place at benefiting their own perspectives of enrichment, the re-enforcing of their power and so on?

You govern in the name of a power, a force that comes from what? From an abstract concept, you have produced a structure you think can be improved upon...But how, in what way has it ever been improved in history? What condition are we are living in today if not a condition of death, of a flattening of quality? This is the critique we need to throw back at the supporters of democracy. If we anarchists are utopians, we are so as a tension towards quality; if democrats are utopians, they are so as a reduction towards quantity. And against reduction, against the atrophy lived in a dimension of the minimum possible damage for them and the maximum damage for the great number of people who are exploited, to this miserable reality we oppose our utopia which is at least a utopia of quality, a tension towards another future, one that will be radically different to what we are living now.

So all the remarks made by anyone who talks to you in the name of political realism, men of State, teachers (who are the servants of men of State), theorists, journalists, all the intellectuals who pass through classrooms like this and in their speechifying talk with the calm, tolerant words of the realist, state that in any case nothing else is possible, reality is what it is, it is necessary to make sacrifices; there, these people are swindling you. They are swindling you because you can do something else, because any one of us is capable of rising up in the name of our wounded dignity before such a swindle. Because any one of us can realize that we have been swindled, because we have finally realized what is being done to our detriment. And in rising up against it all we can change not only the reality of things within the limits that it is possible to know them, but also one's life, make it worthy of being lived. One can get up in the morning, put one's feet on the ground, look in the mirror and say to oneself, "At last I have managed to change things, at least as far as I am concerned" and feel one is a person worthy of living his or her life, not a puppet in the hands of a puppeteer you can't even see well enough to spit in their face.

So that is why anarchists keep coming back to the question of what anarchism is. Because anarchism is not a political movement. Or rather it is, but only in a minor aspect. The fact that the anarchist movement presents itself historically as a political movement does not mean that this exhausts all the anarchist potential for life. Anarchism does not resolve itself in the Cuneo anarchist group, or groups in Turin, London or anywhere else. That is not anarchism. Of course there are anarchists there, or at least one should assume there are, the kind of comrades who have begun their own insurrection individually, have become aware of the context of obligation and coercion that they are forced to live in. But anarchism is not just that, it is also a tension, the quality of life, the strength we manage to draw out of ourselves, the capacity to change the reality of things. Anarchism is the whole of this project of transformation linked to what we produce in ourselves when we bring about our own personal transformation. So it is not a quantifiable fact that can be historicized. Nor is it an event that will simply occur in the course of time, appearing through particular theories, people, movements, as well as, why not, specific revolutionary acts. There is always something more than the sum of these elements, and it is this something more that continues to make anarchism live on in other ways.

So we continually need to maintain a relationship between this tension towards something absolutely other, the unthinkable, the unsayable, a dimension we must achieve without very well knowing how to, and the daily experience of the things we can and do, do. A particular relationship of change, of transformation.

The first example that comes to mind on this question is another contradictory element. Think of the concept behind the statement "there are problems to be solved." This is a classic phrase. We all have problems to solve. Life itself is a problem to be solved. Living is a problem, our social conditions, having to break through the circle that restricts us, right to simple everyday goings on. We consider all this to be a problem.

And herein lies the great misunderstanding. Why? The structures that oppress us (I think many of those present here are students) maintain that problems can be solved and that they can solve them for us. Moreover, they use the example of problems that are solved in geometry, mathematics, etc.. But this kind of problem, the problems of mathematics that are presented as resolvable are false problems, they are not really solved at all. The answers to them are simply a repetition of the same problem in another form, in technical terms, a tautology. One says one thing and answers by repeating the same thing another way. So, basically, the problem is not solved at all, it is merely repeated.

And when we talk of solving a problem that involves the lives of all of us, our daily existence, we are talking of questions of such complexity that they cannot be reduced to a simple restatement of the problem itself. Take, for example, "the problem of the police." The existence of the police constitutes a problem for many of us. There can be no doubt that the policeman is an instrument of repression used by the State to prevent us from doing certain things. How do you solve such a problem? Can the problem of the police be solved? The very question reveals itself to be absurd. There is no such thing as solving the problem of the police. Yet from a democratic point of view it would be possible to solve some aspects by democratizing certain structures, changing policemen's attitudes and so on. Now, to think that this might be a solution to the problem of control and repression would be as stupid as it is illogical. In actual fact, it is nothing other than a way of regulating repression in keeping with the interests of power, of the State. If a democratic politic is effective today, a far less democratic structure of control and repression might be effective in the future just as it has been in the past and any rare, marginal minorities who thought otherwise on the subject would be expelled or eliminated from the ranks.

When I say police, I mean any repressive structure from military police to judiciary, all expressions of the State that serve to control and repress. So, as you can see, social problems cannot be solved. The swindle operated by democratic structures is precisely their claim to solve such problems. This swindle shows how democratic politics are not based on reality or even a minimum of concreteness. Everything is rigged up on the implication that things can be improved, can be resolved in time, can be set right. It is in this concept of setting things right that the strength of power lies, and it is on this improvement that power stands and continues in the medium and long term. Power relations change as we wait for what they promised to come about, but it never does. Because these improvements never materialize. Because power changes and transforms itself throughout history, yet always remains the same. A handful of men, a minority of privileged people who hold the levers of power, look after their own interests and safeguard the conditions of supremacy of whoever happens to be in command.

Now, what instruments do we have to combat this state of affairs? They want to control us? So we refuse control. Of course we can do this. We undoubtedly do, trying to minimize the damage. But to refuse control in a social context is only valid up to a point. We can circumscribe certain aspects of it, yell when we are struck unfairly; but there are clearly certain areas of power where rules are called laws, signposts indicate enclosures, and men calling themselves policemen prevent us from entering. There is no doubt about it, try getting into Parliament and see what happens. I don't know. Certain lines cannot be crossed, certain controls are inevitable.

So what do we do to oppose this situation? Simply dream? Have an idea of freedom, which moreover must be carefully formulated, because we cannot say: "the freedom anarchists want is simply a reduction in control." In that case we would find ourselves faced with the problem: "But where does this reduction in control end?" At a minimal level perhaps? For example, would the State become legitimate for anarchists if instead of being the oppressor State of today, it were to become, let us say, the ideal minimal State of the liberals? No, certainly not. So that is not the way to think. It is not a question of trying to limit control, but of abolishing control altogether. We are not for more freedom. More freedom is given to the slave when his chains are lengthened. We are for the abolition of the chain, so we are for freedom, not more freedom. Freedom means the absence of all chains, the absence of limits and all that ensues from such a statement.

Freedom is a difficult, unknown concept. It is a painful one, yet it is peddled as something beautiful, sweet, relaxing. Like a dream so far off that it makes us feel good, like all the things that, being far off, constitute hope and faith, a belief. In other words, these intangibles which supposedly solve today's problems do not in fact solve them but simply hide them, change them around, preventing us from having a clear vision of all the woes of our times. All right, some day we will be free. Okay, things are a mess, but within this mess there is a subterranean strength, an involuntary order independent of ourselves that works in place of us, which will gradually change the conditions of suffering which we are living in and take us to a free dimension where we will all live happily ever after. No, that is not freedom, that is a swindle that tragically resembles the old idea of God that often helped us, and still helps many people today in their suffering, because they say to themselves, "very well, we are suffering today, but we'll be better off in the next world." In fact, as the Gospel says, the last will be first, heartening the last of today because they see themselves as the first of tomorrow.

If we were to pass off such an idea of freedom as real we would be doing no more than cradling today's suffering by medicating social wounds in exactly the same way as the priest heals those of the poor who listen to his sermon, deceiving themselves that the kingdom of God will save them from their pain. Anarchists cannot think this way. Freedom is a destructive concept that involves the absolute elimination of all limits. Now freedom is an idea we must hold in our hearts, but at the same time we need to understand that if we desire it we must be ready to face all the risks that destruction involves, all the risks of destroying the constituted order we are living under. Freedom is not a concept to cradle ourselves in, in the hope that improvements will develop independently of our real capacity to intervene.

In order to understand such concepts, become aware of the risks one runs by wielding such dangerous concepts, we must be able to form the idea within us.

There is also considerable confusion on this point. It is customary to consider that anything that passes through our minds is an idea. One says "I have an idea" then tries to understand what that means. That is the Cartesian concept of idea as opposed to the Platonic one which is an abstract far off point of reference. But that is not what we are referring to when we say idea. The idea is a point of reference, an element of strength that is capable of transforming life. It is a concept charged with value that becomes a concept of strength, something that can develop and make our relationship with others different. All that is an idea. But what is the source that the elements that make it possible to elaborate such ideas spring from? School, university, newspapers, books, teachers, technicians, television and so on? What reaches us from these instruments of information and cultural elaboration? A considerable accumulation of information cascades down on us, boils inside us like a cauldron, making us produce opinions. We tend not to have ideas, but opinions.

That is the tragic conclusion. What is an opinion? It is a flattened idea, an idea that has been made uniform in order to make it acceptable to the largest number of people. Opinions are massified ideas. It is important for power that these opinions be maintained because it is through opinion, the control of opinion, that they obtain given results, not least the mechanisms of propaganda and electoral procedures through the use of the media. The formation of new power elites comes not from ideas but from opinions.

What does being opposed to opinion-making mean then? Does it mean acquiring more information? That is, opposing counter-information to information? No, that is not possible because no matter how you look at it you cannot possibly oppose the vast amount of information we are bombarded with daily with counter-information capable of "unmasking"through a process of investigating hidden causes, the reality that has been covered up by all that informative chatter. No, we cannot operate in that direction. Whenever we attempt to do so we realize that it is pointless, that we are not able to convince people.

That is why anarchists always consider the problem of propaganda critically: Yes, of course, as you see there is a well-stocked table here as is always the case at initiatives or conferences of this kind. There are always our pamphlets, our books. We are laden with papers and are very good at bringing out such publications. But that is not the only kind of work we need to do, and in any case they do not contain elements of counter-information, or if they do it is purely accidental. This work is aimed essentially, or should be, at building an idea or a number of leading ideas, a number of strong ideas.

Let us give just one example. Over the past three or four years an affair has developed that the newspapers have reported using horrible terms like *"tangentopoli"* or "clean hands" [legal proceedings in which many politicians were convicted for having accepted money from capitalists in exchange for contracts in the public works sector] and so on. Now what has this operation instilled in people's minds? It has built the opinion that the law is capable of setting things right, of sentencing politicians, changing conditions, so can take us from the old concepts typical of the first Italian Republic to the new ones of the Second Republic. This opinion, this process, is clearly very useful. For example it has allowed the emergence of a "new" power elite to take the place of the old. New up to a point, but with certain characteristics and sad rehashes of old habits and personages. This is the way opinion functions.

Now, consider comparing this process of opinion-making, which is of considerable advantage to power alone, to the construction of an idea-force that might be an in-depth analysis of the concept of justice. The difference is abyssal. But what is right? For example, it was certainly right for many, and we also considered it right ourselves, for ex-Socialist Party leader [Bettino] Craxi to be forced to remain locked up in his villa in Tunisia. The whole thing has been quite amusing, it even made us laugh, made us feel good because it is quite nice when pigs at that level end up being put out of circulation. But is that real justice? For example, [Giulio] Andreotti is in trouble. It seems he kissed [Salvatore] Riina (mafia boss) on the cheek.

Such news certainly makes us smile, makes us feel better, because a pig like Andreotti was annoying even at a simple physical level, just seeing him on TV was enough. But what is this idea of justice? Judges for the prosecution Di Pietro and Borrelli have a horde of supporting fans. Millions of people have been drawn into this process of uniforming opinion.

Is the concept of justice we need to ponder any different? What should it lead to? It should lead us to recognize that if Craxi or Andreotti are responsible then people like Di Pietro or Borrelli are responsible to the same extent. Because if the former are politicians, the others are all magistrates. The concept of justice means fixing a demarcation line between those who support and defend power and those who are against it. If the very existence of power is unjust and if all attempts, some of which we have just seen, reveal themselves to be no more than self-justifying swindles, any man of power, more or less democratic as he might be, always stands on the wrong side of justice no matter what he does.

To build such a concept of justice obviously means to form an idea, an idea you don't find in the newspapers, that isn't covered in the classrooms or university auditoriums, which cannot become an element of opinion or lead people to vote. In fact, such an idea leads to internal conflict. Because before the tribunal of one's self one asks, "But I, with my idea of social justice, how do I see it when what Di Pietro does seems good? Am I being taken for a ride too? Am I also an instrument of opinion, a terminal of the great processes for maintaining power, becoming not just their slave but also their accomplice?"

We have finally got there. We have reached the point of our own responsibility. Because if it is true that for anarchists there is no difference between theory and action, as soon as the idea of social justice lights up in us, illuminates our brain even for a split second, it will never be able to extinguish itself again. Because no matter what we think, we will feel guilty, will feel we are accomplices, accomplices to a process of discrimination, repression, genocide, death, a process we will never be able to feel detached from again. How could we define ourselves revolutionaries and anarchists otherwise? What freedom would we be supporting if we were to give our complicity to the assassins in power?

You see how different and critical the situation is for whoever succeeds, through deep analysis of reality or simply by chance or misfortune, in letting an idea as clear as the idea of justice penetrate their brain? There are many such ideas. For example, the idea of freedom is similar. Anyone who thinks about what freedom actually is even for a moment will never again be able to content themselves by simply doing something to slightly extend the freedom of the situations they are living in. From that moment on they will feel guilty and will try to do something to alleviate their sense of suffering. They will fear they have done wrong by not having done anything until now, and from that moment on their lives will change completely.

Basically, what does the State want from the formation of opinion? What does power want? Yes, of course, it wants to create mass opinion because from that they are able to carry out certain operations such as voting, the formation of power groups and so on. But that is not all they want. They want our consent. They want our approval. And consent is gained through precise instruments, especially those of a cultural nature. For example, school is one of the reservoirs from which consent is produced and the future intellectual, though not just intellectual, workforce is built.

Today capitalism requires a different kind of person to those it required in the past. Up until recently there was a need for people with professional capacities, a pride in this capacity and particular qualifications. The situation is quite different now. The world of work requires a very modest qualification level whereas qualities that did not exist and were even inconceivable in the past such as flexibility, adaptability, tolerance, the capacity to intervene at meetings, etc. are required in their place.

Huge production units based on assembly lines for example now use robots or are built on the conceptual basis of islands, small groups working together who know each other and control each other and so on. This kind of mentality is not only found in the factory. It is not just a "new worker" they are building, but a "new man"; a flexible person with modest ideas, rather opaque in their desires, with considerably reduced cultural levels, impoverished language, standardized reading, a limited capacity to think and a great capacity to make quick yes or no decisions. They know how to choose between two possibilities: a yellow button, a red button, a black button, a white button. This is the kind of mentality they are building. And where are they building it? At school, but also in everyday life.

What will they do with such a person? They will use them to bring about all the modifications that are necessary for restructuring capital. They will be useful for a better management of the conditions and relations of the capitalism of tomorrow. And what will these relations be? They will be based on faster and faster change, a call to satisfying non-existent desires, desires that are piloted, determined by small groups that are becoming more and more numerous. This new person is quite the opposite of what we are capable of imagining or desiring, the opposite of quality, creativity, the opposite of real desire, the joy of life, the opposite of all this. How can we fight against the construction of this technological man? How can we struggle against this situation? Can we wait for a day to come, a great day that will turn the world upside down? What the anarchists of the last century called "*la grande soirée*"? The great evening or the great day—"*le grand jour*"—in which forces no one could foresee would end up taking over, exploding into that social conflict we are all waiting for, called revolution? So everything will change and there will be a world of perfection and joy?

This is a millenarian idea. Now that we are reaching the end of the millennium it could take root again. But conditions have changed. This is not reality, it is not this waiting that interests us. What does interest us is another kind of intervention, a far more modest one, but one that is capable of achieving something. As anarchists we are called to do something. We are called by our own individual responsibility and by what we said earlier. From the moment the idea lights up our mind, not the idea of anarchy, but of justice, freedom, when these ideas illuminate our minds and we see the swindle before us—which today more than ever before we can define a democratic swindle—what can we do? We must set to work, and this setting to work also means organizing ourselves. It means creating conditions that foster relationships among anarchists, conditions that must be different than those of the past.

Reality has changed. As I said before, they are building a different man, a de-skilled man, and they are building him because they need to build a de-skilled society. They have removed the figure of the worker from the center of the conception of the political society as it was, after de-skilling him. In the past the worker bore the greatest brunt of exploitation. That is why it was thought that this social figure would necessarily give birth to the revolution. It is sufficient to think of the Marxist analysis. Marx's *Capital* is dedicated to the "liberation" of the worker. When Marx speaks of man, he means the worker. In his analysis of value, he is speaking of the work pace; in his analysis of alienation, he is talking about work. There is nothing that does not concern work. But that is because the worker was central to the Marxist analysis at the time when it was developed. The working class could be seen to be the center of the social structure.

Using different analyses, anarchists also came close to an account that the worker's position was the center of the social world. Think of the anarcho-syndicalist analyses. For the anar-cho-syndicalists it was a question of taking the concept of trade union struggle to its extreme consequences, freeing it from the narrower dimension of trade union bargaining and developing it right to the production of the revolution through the general strike. So according to the anarcho-syndicalists the Society of the future, the free anarchist Society, was to be nothing other than the present Society freed from power but with the same productive structures, no longer in the hands of the capitalists but in the hands of the collective which would manage them in common.

This concept is quite impracticable today for various rea-sons. First of all, because technological transformation has made it impossible for there to be a simple passage from the present society to the future one we desire to live in. A direct passage would be impossible for the simple reason that it is not possible to use information technology in liberated forms, in a liberatory way. The new technologies and computer tech-nology applications have not limited themselves to bringing about certain modifications in particular instruments, they have transformed all the other technologies as well. The fac-tory, for instance, is not simply a structure of the past with the addition of computer technology but has become a computer-ized factory, which is quite different. Bearing this in mind we can only mention these concepts in a very general way because it would take time to go into them adequately. So we must recognize that it is not possible to use this patrimony. This passage runs parallel to the end of the myth of the centrality of the working class.

Now, in a situation where the working class has practically disintegrated, the possibility of an expropriation of the means of production no longer exists. So what is the conclusion? The only possible conclusion is that this set of instruments of pro-duction we have before us be destroyed. The only possible way is to pass through the dramatic reality of destruction. If the revolution we imagine and which moreover we cannot be cer-tain will ever come about, it will not be the revolution of the past that saw itself as one single event that might even take place in a day or one fine evening but will be a long, tragic, bloody affair that could pass through inconceivably violent, inconceivably tragic processes.

All this is the kind of reality we are moving towards. Not because that is what we desire, not because we like violence, blood, destruction, civil war, death, rape, barbarity. It is not that, but because it is the only plausible road, the road that the transformation wanted by those ruling us and who are in command have made necessary. They have moved on to this road. We cannot change all that with a simple flight of fancy, a simple dream. In the past hypothesis where a strong working class existed, one could fool oneself about this passage and organize accordingly. For example, the organizational proposal of anarcho-syndicalism saw a strong syndicalist movement which, penetrating the working class and organizing almost the whole of it, was to bring about this expropriation and passage. This collective subject, who was probably mythical from the start, no longer exists even in its mythical version, so what sense would there be in a syndicalist movement of a revolutionary nature? What sense would there be in an anarcho-syndicalist movement? None at all.

So the struggle must begin elsewhere, with other ideas and methods. That is why we have been developing a critique of syndicalism and anarcho-syndicalism for about fifteen years. That is why we are, and define ourselves, insurrectionary anarchists. Not because we think the solution is the barricades—the barricades could be a tragic consequence of choices that are not our own—but we are insurrectionaries because we think that anarchist action must necessarily face very serious problems. These problems are not desired by anarchism but are imposed by the reality that those in power have built, and we cannot obliterate them simply by wishing them away.

An anarchist organization that projects itself into the future should therefore be agile. It cannot present itself with the cumbersome characteristics and quantitative heaviness of the structures of the past. It cannot present itself in a dimension of synthesis like organizations of the past where the anarchist structures claimed to sum up reality in "commissions" that treated all the various problems, making decisions at periodic congresses on the basis of theses that belong to the last century. All this has seen its day, not because a century has passed since it was thought out, but because reality has changed.

That is why we maintain that there is a need for the formation of small groups based on the concept of affinity, even tiny groups made up of a small number of comrades who know each other and deepen this knowledge because there cannot be affinity if one does not have knowledge of the other. One can only recognize one's affinities by going into the elements that determine one's differences, by spending time with each other. This knowledge is a personal fact, but it is also a question of ideas, debate, discussions. But in relation to the first points we made this evening, if you remember, there can be no going into ideas if there is not also a practice of carrying out actions. So, there is a continual reciprocal process of going into ideas and carrying out actions.

A small group of comrades, a small group who simply meet in the evening to have a chat would not be an affinity group but a group of friends, pub mates who meet in the evenings to talk about anything under the sun. On the contrary, a group that meets to discuss things and in discussing prepares itself for *doing*, and through that doing contributes to developing discussion that transforms itself into discussion about things to be done, this is the mechanism of the affinity group. So how then can affinity groups enter into contact with others where the deepened knowledge that exists in the single group does not necessarily exist? This contact can be assured by informal organization.

But what is an informal organization? There could be relationships of an informal kind between the various affinity groups that enter into contact with each other in order to exchange ideas and do things together, and consequently the existence of an organization, also very widespread throughout the country, comprised of even tens, or why not, hundreds of organizations, structures, groups of an informal character based on discussion, periodic analyses, things to be done together, etc. The organizational logic of insurrectionary anarchism is different from the organizations we mentioned earlier concerning anar-cho-syndicalism. The organizational forms referred to here in a few words merit going into, something I cannot do now in the context of a conference. But such a way of organizing would, in my opinion, remain simply something within the anarchist movement were it not also to produce relations beyond it, that is through the construction of external groups, external nuclei, also with informal characteristics. These groups should not be composed of anarchists alone, anyone who intends to struggle to reach given objectives, even circumscribed ones, could par-ticipate so long as they take a number of essential conditions into account. First of all, permanent conflict, that is groups with the characteristic of attacking the reality in which they find themselves without waiting for orders from anywhere else. Then the characteristic of being "autonomous," that is of not depending on or having any relations at all with political par-ties or trade union organizations. Finally, the characteristic of facing problems one by one and not proposing platforms of generic claims that would inevitably transform themselves into administration along the lines of a mini-party or a small alter-native trade union. The summary of these ideas might seem rather abstract and that is why before ending I would like to give an example, because some of these things can be better understood in practice.

A theoretical model of this kind was used in an attempt to prevent the construction of the American missile base in Comiso in the early 1980s. The anarchists who intervened for two years built "self-managed leagues." These self-managed leagues were specifically non-anarchist groups that operated in the area with the unique aim of preventing the construction of the base by destroying the project during construction.

The leagues were autonomous nuclei characterized by the fact that their only aim was to attack and destroy the base. They did not take on a whole series of problems, because if they had they would have become groups of syndicalists with the aim of, let us say, defending jobs, or finding work, or resolv-ing other immediate problems. Instead, their sole aim was to destroy the base. The second characteristic was permanent conflict, i.e., from the moment these groups were formed (they were not specifically anarchist groups, but there were people in them who were anarchists), they went into conflict with all the forces involved in building the base, without this conflict being determined or declared by any representative organism or by the anarchists who had promoted the initiative. The third characteristic was the complete autonomy of these groups, that is to say they did not have links with any parties or unions, etc. We only have partial knowledge of the struggle against the base. And I don't know if it makes sense to take up the story again here, I just wanted to mention it as an example.

So insurrectionary anarchism must overcome one essential problem. It must go beyond a certain limit otherwise it will remain no more than the idea of insurrectionary anarchism. That is, the comrades who have lived an insurrection of a personal nature we mentioned earlier, that illumination which produces an idea-force inside us in opposition to the chatter of opinion, and form affinity groups, enter into relationships with comrades from other places through an informal kind of structure, only realize a part of the work. At a certain point they must decide, must go beyond the demarcation line, take a step that it isn't easy to turn back from. They must enter into a relationship with people that are not anarchists concerning a problem that is intermediate, circumscribed (such as, for example the destruction of the base in Comiso). No matter how fantastic or interesting this idea might have been it certainly wasn't the achievement of anarchy. What would have happened if one had really managed to enter the base and destroy it? I don't know. Probably nothing, possibly everything. I don't know, no one can tell. But the beauty of carrying out the destructive event is not to be found in its possible consequences.

Anarchists guarantee none of the things they do. They point out the responsibility of individuals and structures on the basis of the decision that they are determined to act, and from that moment on they feel sure of themselves because their idea of justice informs their action. It points at one person's responsibility, or that of more people, one structure or more structures, and the consequences that such responsibility leads to. It is here that we find anarchists' determination to act.

But once they act along with other people, they must also try to build organisms that are capable of holding together and imposing consequences in the struggle against power. We must never forget this. And this is an important point to reflect upon: power reproduces itself in time and space, it is not something abstract. Control would not be possible if police stations did not exist, if prisons did not exist. Legislative power would not be possible if parliament did not exist, or if there were no little regional parliaments. The cultural power that oppresses us, that fabricates opinion, would not be possible if there were no schools and universities. Now, schools, universities, police stations, prisons, industries, factories, are all things that reproduce themselves in specific places, in circumscribed areas which we can only move around in if we accept given conditions and play the game. We are here at the moment because we agreed to play the game. We would not have been able to enter the building otherwise. This is interesting. We can use structures of this kind. But at the time of attack such places are forbidden to us. If we were to have come in here with the intent of attacking, the police would obviously have prevented us.

Now, because power reproduces itself in physical space, anarchists' relation to this is important. Of course insurrection is an individual fact and so in that place deep inside us, at night as we are about to go to sleep, we think "...well, in the last analysis things aren't too bad," one feels at peace with oneself and falls asleep. There, in that particular place inside us, that private space, we can move about as we please. But then we must transfer ourselves into the physical space of social reality. And physical space, when you think about it, is almost exclusively under the control of power. So, when we move about in this space we carry this value of insurrection with us, these revolutionary values, and measure them in a clash in which we are not the only ones present.

We must therefore individuate significant objectives and verify their existence—and as luck would have it these objectives exist perpetually, everywhere—contribute to creating the conditions so that people, the exploited on whose backs these objectives are built, do something to destroy them.

I believe this revolutionary process is of an insurrectionary nature. It does not have aims (and this is important) of a quantitative nature, because the destruction of an objective or the prevention of a project cannot be measured in quantitative terms. It sometimes happens that someone says to me, "But what results have we obtained?" When something is done, people don't even remember the anarchists afterwards. "Anarchists? Who are these anarchists? Monarchists? Are they these people who support the king?" People don't remember very well. But what does it matter? It is not us that they must remember, but their struggle, because the struggle is theirs, we are simply an option in that struggle. We are something extra.

In the freed society where anarchy has been reached in an ideal manner, anarchists, who are indispensable in the social struggle at all levels, would simply have the role of pushing struggles further and further, eliminating even the smallest traces of power and always perfecting the tension towards anarchy. Anarchists inhabit an uncomfortable world in any case because when the struggle is going well they are forgotten about and when the struggle goes badly they are accused of being responsible, of having approached it the wrong way, of having taken it to the wrong conclusions. No illusion then concerning any quantitative results: if the struggle maintained from an insurrectionary point of view is correct, has gone well, the results if any might be useful to the people who brought it about, certainly not to the anarchists. It is important not to fall prey to the illusion that many anarchists unfortunately do, of believing that the positive outcome of a struggle can result in a growth in our groups, because that is not so and this systematically leads to disillusion. The growth of our groups and an increase in the number of comrades is important but that does not come about from the results obtained so much as through the building, the formation, of this idea-force, the clarification we talked about earlier. The positive results of struggles and the numerical growth in anarchist groups are two things that cannot be seen as a process of cause and effect. They might be connected, they might not.

Just a couple of words to wind up, I have talked about what anarchism is, what democracy is, and the misconceptions we are constantly being faced with; of the ways the structures of power we call modern capitalism, post-industrial capitalism, are being transformed; of some anarchist structures of struggle that are no longer acceptable today and the way one can oppose oneself to the reality of power and, finally, I mentioned the difference between traditional anarchism and the insurrectional anarchism of the present day.

Thank you.

THE INSURRECTIONARY PROJECT

IF WE REFUSE TO LET OUR LIVES BE ORGANIZED BY OTHERS WE must have the capacity to organize ourselves, that is, we must be able to "put together the elements necessary to act as a coherent functioning whole." For anarchists, individuals who ardently desire the elimination of every trace of tyranny and domestication, this has been experimented with in a myriad of forms according to prevailing social and economic conditions, and marked by each one's particular concept of wholeness. If this could once be interpreted—by some—to mean a big organization to oppose big industry, today social disintegration and uncertainty have gone further than any critique in relegating such undertakings to the pages of history. We are left with the exquisite dilemma: if my freedom depends on the freedom of all, does not the freedom of all depend on my acting to free myself? And if all the exploited are not acting to free themselves—as a tangible composite whole—how can I function, i.e. organize myself, to destroy the reality that oppresses me without delay? In other words, how can I act as a whole that seeks to expand and enhance itself to infinity? Having refused the sop of participation, voluntary work, and progressive change with which the democratic ideology seeks to satiate its bloated subjects, I am left with myself and my unmediated strength. I seek my accomplices: two or three, hundreds or hundreds of thousands, to upset and attack the present social order right now—in the tiny act that gives immediate joy, indicating that sabotage is possible for everyone; or in great moments of mass destruction where creativity and anger combine in unpredictable collusion. I am therefore faced with the problem of creating a project whose immediate aim is destruction, which in turn creates space for the new.

What holds things together and puts my actions in context cannot therefore be a fixed formal organization, but the development of the capacity to organize myself, alone and with others, where numbers are not an aim, but are always potentially present. In other words, I must create an insurrectional project which already contains all the elements of a revolutionary perspective: the decision to act now; analysis of the present time taking account of the profound transformations Capital is undergoing globally and which have had an effect on the whole concept of struggle; choice of objectives, means, ideas, desires; the means of making these known to others in my search for affinity; the creation of occasions for confrontation and debate, and much more besides. Projectuality becomes force in movement, a propelling element within the whole insurrectional flux.

The following texts come to us from a series of meetings that took place in Greece some years ago. A sub-heading of one of the sections has since reached notoriety after being chosen by the Italian carabinieri in 1996 to name the phantom armed organization they subsequently accused dozens of anarchists of belonging to. This should not divert us from our understanding of the text, which could be seen as a starting point, an invitation to consider and experiment in the insurrectional adventure.

Jean Weir

IN JANUARY 1993 I WAS INVITED TO GREECE ALONG WITH another comrade to hold a number of talks at the Athens Polytechnic and the Law Faculty of Salonika.

The texts published here are: an outline of the talks I intended to give, a transcription of the tapes of the Salonika conference and a transcription of an interview with the Athens daily *Eleftherotipia*. As the first of these texts was intended to be a guide to the conferences, I worked it out in detail along with the Greek comrades in time for it to be translated and handed out to those present. This was necessary due to the difficulties of on the spot interpretation.

I published the texts in May 1993 in issue 72 of *Anarchismo*, with the title "Recent Developments in Capitalism."

The three pieces have a homogeneity that still makes them worth publishing together, as they all concern capitalist restructuring and the forms of insurrectionary struggle that anarchists are proposing against it.

A curious thing happened. The penultimate section of the first piece published here is still entitled "Revolutionary anarchist insurrectionary organization." The origin of this now infamous heading is rather strange and deserves comment. In fact I had originally entitled the subsection "Informal anarchist insurrectionary organization," but we came up against difficulties when trying to translate the term "informal." It was impossible to solve them before my arrival in Greece, so the comrades suggested replacing the term "informal" with the more generic one, "revolutionary."

I forgot to restore the word "informal" when I published the text in Italy, although it is nearer to what I am talking about in that particular section.

I do not feel I can make such a correction now given all the nonsense that the specialists of the Attorney General's office in the courts of Rome, led by Public Prosecutor Marini, have come out with.

I think it might be useful to give a brief description of the way the minds of the Italian judiciary and Carabinieri have labored on this text.

On September 17, 1997, dozens of anarchists were arrested in Italy on charges of kidnapping, robbery, murder, possession of arms, etc., initiating what came to be known as the "Marini Frame-up." These separate charges were transformed into one combined charge, i.e. that of belonging to a clandestine armed organization entitled the ORAI. The name had been taken from the paragraph mentioned above: Revolutionary anarchist insurrectionary organization.

This trial is still going on, and could drag on for years to come[1] given the various legal stages which make up the process. We were freed from prison fourteen months after being arrested thanks to a simple procedural error: the Attorney's Office genius in Rome had been so busy trying to justify a phantom "armed gang" that they forgot to follow their own rules. The result is that although still facing charges that carry life imprisonment, those who, like myself, did not have sentences pending are now all at liberty.

As the enthralled reader will discover, the following texts contain no theory relative to a specific armed organization, but

1   Bonanno would finally be sentenced for his role ten years later, in 2003. — *Detritus*

are an examination of the insurrectionary method of organizing. This is based on affinity groups composed of anarchists, the elaboration of a common revolutionary project, their linking together in an informal organization, the constitution of base nuclei in a situation of mass struggle and, finally, the way these structures could be linked together.

I realize that for the obtuse mentality of a Carabinieri taught to see the enemy as a mirror image of himself and his organization, nothing under the sun could exist that is not equipped with an organization chart, leaders, strategies, and objectives. And up to this point I can even understand a tendentious reading of the text in question. But what I cannot understand, and what no reader will surely be able to either, is how such a text came to be given the task of constituting the foundations of a clandestine armed organization. This is still simmering away in the mind of the Public Prosecutor, who will stop at nothing to demonstrate our guilt.

Stop at nothing. Precisely, even to the point of denying all the evidence to the contrary. And in fact, as appears from the trial documents and even from the succinct phrasing of the arrest warrants, they must have had a few doubts on the subject. However, these were evidently cast aside due to the greater precedence of their need to justify the unjustifiable: *If it is true that Bonanno is theorizing a specific armed clandestine organization (ORAI) in this piece ("Recent Developments in Capitalism"), then we, the Prosecution and Carabinieri, declare that he cannot have gone to Greece to talk about it publicly in a university auditorium. That would be illogical. And as the text in question must mean what we, Prosecution and Carabinieri, say it means, then we must conclude that Bonanno did not go to Greece, did not give these conferences, and did not write this text as an outline and memorandum for what he was about to say in public...A logical conclusion!* But it ignores one thing: that in both Athens and Salonika hundreds of people were present at these conferences. There are tape recordings not just of the conferences but of the whole debate. Both the conferences and the Salonika debate have been transcribed and presented in a book published in Greece. And, finally, there are even photographs published along with my interview (the third of the pieces published here) on February 28 1993 in the Athens daily *Eleftherotipia*.

But why does the prosecution want to read something— the theorization of an inexistent armed band complete with a name—into this text, even at the risk of making themselves look ridiculous? There is a simple answer: because they would not otherwise be able to sentence dozens of anarchists for conspiracy—a conspiracy that clearly does not exist. It would then remain for them only to prove individual charges which would have to be dealt with separately, according to the rules of the penal code, etc.

The accusers know perfectly well that the second option would not be easy for them. They are well aware that most of the charges are based on the spurious accusations of a young girl bribed by them, *that* is why they are so persistent in wanting to read something in this text that is not there.

In fact, the concept of informal organization proposed in the text in question does not in any way resemble that of an armed clandestine organization. We are in two different worlds. The closed organization (necessarily so if we are talking of *clandestinity*), is an instrument like any other, and in certain conditions of the class struggle it might even be useful as defensive or offensive means if one finds oneself in dire straits. The economic and social structure would have to change profoundly in order for it to become useful as a means today. Capital would have to turn back on its steps to the conditions of production that existed in the 1980s when there was a strong centralized working class and a fixed transmission belt of left wing unions and parties—all things which clearly no longer exist. The closed organizational model, which only indirectly wants the struggle to generalize and does nothing in that direction other than make its actions known through the media—and we know how *that* functions—corresponds in many respects to the ideological conditions that sum up the union and the party. If we refuse to be likened to political parties, we must also refuse to be compared to organizations whose aim is numerical growth, increasing the number of its actions and setting itself up as the mainstay of the class struggle.

Of course, if anarchists were to get involved in constituting a specific, closed organization, they would do it in quite a different way than the classic sclerotic one of the Marxist-Leninists. And there is no doubt that, in its time, *Azione Rivoluzionaria*[2] was an attempt in that direction. But it soon moved away from its initial trajectory in the direction of a generalization of the struggle, and closed itself up in the logic of recruiting and joining arms with the other combatant organizations on the scene at the time. I am not saying that they did not make any interesting proposals, especially in their early documents. What I am saying is that, not only did these proposals not stand up to criticism but by withdrawing into a position of defense they ended up annihilating themselves by becoming more and more clandestine, that's all. The best comrades, it was said at the time, are those in prison. One simply had to end up in prison to become a better comrade.

The problem is simple. When we work out an analysis we cannot put our own personal positions aside. These inevitably come to permeate the analysis without our meaning it to. And when the latter is written in prison, it is obvious that that is where it has come from. Moreover, when a comrade sees his immediate reality to be radically compromised he conveys this in the analyses he is working on, as well as in the kind of intervention and methods he proposes. By imprisoning himself in the stifling viewpoint of a clandestine organization his way of thinking becomes clandestine even to himself, almost without realizing it.

It has been said that if one were to find oneself in a pre-revolutionary phase (although no one could explain how we were to recognize this phase), the only road possible would be that of the more or less closed armed organization. It was later seen that all attempts at "being different" simply ended up aborting themselves in the classic condition of closure. It does not occur to anyone today that we are in a pre-revolutionary phase, so if

2   Anarchist guerrilla group formed in 1977, influenced by the Situationists and the German June 2 Movement, disbanded within just a few years. — *Detritus*

we were to accept the idea of a specific armed organization it would simply be a question of our own personal decision, nothing more. A choice like any other. And I say that with no expectations concerning the accusations in the trial in Rome.

At this point I could quote something I wrote years ago, in an article published in *Anarchismo*—in 1979 to be exact—entitled "On Clandestine Organization," which is also available in my book *La rivoluzione illogica* (*The Illogical Revolution*), but it seems pointless to me. While many might simply have forgotten these words from the past, I myself do not know what to do with them. I do not even want to read them again, because they belong to a period that is quite different from the present. As far as I can remember, they referred to the fact that the critique of the closed clandestine organization is not simply an affirmation of individualism. Criticism does not have a weakening effect, it strengthens. But something strange occurs when those under criticism are comrades who participate in, or support, a closed form of organization, even in theory. The critique is taken as a personal attack or something aimed at weakening one's conditions. And when you are faced with a comrade with years of prison hanging over them, you run the risk of being lynched. I do not think that the concept of the generalization of the struggle, including armed struggle, is the refusal of organization. Nor do I think that to criticize the closed clandestine organization means to "subject oneself to massacre." Such generalizations do not interest me.

The informal organization of affinity groups and the consequent development of base nuclei in specific mass struggles, are the organizational forms I consider most useful today for the generalization of the struggle, armed or otherwise.

Alfredo M. Bonanno
Catania, October 10, 1998

FROM THE LATE 1970S UNTIL THE EARLY 1980S, INDUSTRY IN the leading capitalist countries was in crisis. The relationship between factory and productivity had never been worse. Struggles led by the trade unions, as well as those of the proletariat in general (especially in their more violent manifestations under the leadership of the various revolutionary working class structures), had led to a rise in labor costs quite out of proportion to Capital's profits. Incapable of adjusting, lacking the strength to reduce labor and employment costs drastically, it seemed as though the whole system was moving towards its natural collapse.

But by the first half of the 1980s rapid change had set in, with industrial restructuring taking a sharp turn towards automation. The primary and secondary productive sectors (industry and agriculture) were in decline, with consequent reductions in employment. The tertiary (services) sector had expanded out of all proportion, absorbing some of the laid-off work force, thus attenuating the social backlash that the capitalists had feared more than anything else.

In short, the much-feared riots and revolutions did not take place. There was no intolerable pressure from the reserve army of the proletariat. Instead, everything quietly adapted to changes in the structures of production.

Heavy industry replaced old factories with automated ones capable of reaching hitherto undreamed of levels of flexibility and low levels of investment. Labor costs decreased without this leading to any fall in demand because the services sector held well, assuring levels of income that were sufficient to inflate the capitalist system as a whole. Most of the laid off workers managed to find some way of getting by in the new flexible and permissive capitalist world.

THE NEW PRODUCTIVE AND DEMOCRATIC MENTALITY

None of this would have been possible without the emergence of a new flexible mentality at the work place: a reduction in the need for professional qualifications and an increase in the demand for small, auxiliary jobs. This coincided with a consolidation of the democratic mentality.

The middle classes' myths of careers and improvements in workers' wages disappeared for good. All this was possible thanks to articulated interventions at every level:

1. In the schools, in the adoption of less rigid teaching methods better suited to building a "malleable" personality in young people. This was to enable them to adapt to an uncertain future of the kind that would have filled their parents with horror;

2. In the political management of the most advanced capitalist countries. Authoritarianism gave way to democratization, involving people in fictitious electoral and referenda procedures;

3. In production where, as we have said, the disappearance of professional qualifications has made producers tame and flexible.

This all took place according to the spirit of the times. Dreams of philosophical and scientific certainty gave way to a "weak" model, based not on risk and courage but on adjustment in the short-term, on the principle that nothing is certain but anything can be fixed.

As well as contributing to the disappearance of the old and in many aspects out-of-date, authoritarianism, the democratic mentality also led to a tendency to compromise at every level. This resulted in a moral degradation where the dignity of the oppressed was exchanged for a guaranteed but uncomfortable survival. Struggles receded and weakened.

OBSTACLES FACED BY THE INSURRECTIONARY STRUGGLE AGAINST POST-INDUSTRIAL CAPITALISM AND THE STATE

Undoubtedly one obstacle to be faced is precisely this amorphous, flexible mentality outlined above. This cannot be compared to the old-style reliance on social security; it is simply a desire to find a niche in which to survive, work as little as possible, accept all the rules of the system and disdain ideals and projects, dreams and utopias. The laboratories of Capital have done an exemplary job in this sense. School, factory, culture, and sport have united to produce individuals who are domesticated in every respect, incapable of suffering or knowing their enemies, unable to dream, desire, struggle, or act to transform reality.

Another obstacle, which is related to the first, consists of pushing production to the margins of the post-industrial complex as a whole. The dismembering of the class of producers is no longer a nebulous project, it has become a reality. And the division into numerous small sectors which often work against each other is increasing this marginalization.

This is fast making the traditional structures of worker resistance, such as workers' parties and trade unions, obsolete. Recent years have witnessed a progressive disappearance of the old-style trade unionism, including that which once aspired to revolution and self-management. But, more importantly, we have witnessed the collapse of the Communism which claimed to have built a socialist State—built with police control and ideological repression.

It cannot be said that any organizational strategy capable of responding to the new conditions of capitalist productive and social reality in general has emerged.

Developments that might have arisen from proposals made by insurrectionary anarchists, especially those moving in the direction of informal relations between individuals and groups based on affinity, have not yet been fully taken on board. They have often received a tepid welcome by comrades due to a certain, in some ways understandable, reluctance to abandon the old ways of thinking and apply new methods of organization.

We will say something about this further on as it is central to the struggle against the new structures of repression and total control produced by Capital and the State.

RESTRUCTURING TECHNOLOGY

The present technological revolution based on information technology, lasers, the atom, subatomic particles, new materials such as fiber optics which allow energy transportation and consumption at speeds and over distances once unthinkable, genetic modification concerning not only agriculture and animals but also people, etc., has not stopped at changing the world. It has done more. It has produced conditions that make it seem impossible to plan or make plans for the foreseeable future, not only as far as those who intend to maintain the present state of affairs are concerned, but also by those who intend to destroy them.

The main reason for this is that the new technologies, which are now interacting and becoming part of the context that has been developing over at least the past 2,000 years, could produce unpredictable results. And some of these results could be totally destructive, far beyond the devastating effects of an atomic explosion.

Hence the need for a project aimed at the destruction of technology as a whole in its first, essential phase, and which bases all its political and social approaches on this imperative.

Profound changes are also taking place in the economic sector. These changes are affecting the political situation in advanced capitalist countries, with consequent effects on the military sector.

New frontiers in post-industrial capitalism are emerging from widespread processes and rearrangements that are continually in flux. The static concept of production tied to heavy machinery in huge factories capable of producing a multiplicity of consumer goods has been surpassed by the ingenious idea of rapid change and increasing competition in specialized production with stylish, individual, personalized products. The post-industrial product does not require skilled labor but is set up on the production line directly, simply by reprogramming the robots to produce it. This has meant incredible reduction in storage and distribution costs and eliminated obsolescence and stockpiling of unsold products.

This development created great new possibilities for Capital around the beginning of the 1980s, and by the end of the decade it had become the norm. So the political situation had to change to correspond with the new economic one.

This explains the considerable changes that took place at the end of the 1980s and the beginning of the 1990s. There has been a move towards careful selection of the managerial strata, which must be able to see to the requirements of this new form of production. That explains why advanced industrial countries such as the US and Great Britain went through a period of increased authoritarianism in government, then moved on to a more versatile, flexible form of political management corresponding to the economic necessities of various countries which are now all coordinated globally.

THE COLLAPSE OF "ACTUALLY EXISTING SOCIALISM" AND THE REBIRTH OF VARIOUS FORMS OF NATIONALISM

Any advance from the countries of "actually existing socialism" beyond cautious, reciprocal suspicion was unthinkable in the old capitalist reality. But the birth of the new computerized, automated capitalism has not only made advances possible but has forced these countries to change radically, pushing them to an irreversible, as it was nasty, collapse.

Rigid authoritarian regimes based on ideological jokes such as proletarian internationalism and the like are finding it difficult to comply with the needs imposed by a production structure that is now coordinated globally.

If they do not want to get stuck in a precarious, marginal situation, the few remaining authoritarian regimes will have to resolutely democratize their political management. Inflexibility forces the great international partners of industrial development to stiffen and declare war one way or the other.

It is in this sense that the role of the army has also changed considerably. It has intensified internal repression, and at the same time taken on the role of global policeman that was first developed by the US. This will probably continue for a number of years until other crises interrupt and require new yet equally precarious and dangerous forms of equilibrium.

Accordingly, the resurgence of nationalism is bringing with it one positive albeit limited element, and one that is extremely dangerous. Its immediate and specific effect consists in the overturning and dismemberment of the big States. Any movement that goes in this direction is to be hailed as positive, even if on the surface it presents itself as being a carrier of traditional, conservative values.

The other factor, the one that is extremely dangerous, is the risk of wars spreading between the small States, declared and fought with unprecedented ferocity and causing tremendous suffering in the name of miserable principles and just as miserable alternatives.

Many of these wars will lead to a more efficient and structured form of post-industrial capitalism. Many will be controlled and piloted by the multinational giants themselves. But basically they represent a transitory condition, a kind of epileptic fit, following which social conditions could evolve in the direction of the elimination of any trace of the old State organisms.

At the moment we can only guess how this might happen, starting off from an examination of conditions today.

POSSIBLE DEVELOPMENTS OF THE INSURRECTIONARY MASS
STRUGGLE IN THE DIRECTION OF ANARCHIST COMMUNISM

The end of the great trade union organizations' function of resistance and defense—corresponding with the collapse of the working class—has allowed us to see another possibility for the organization of the struggle. This could start from the real capacity of the *excluded*, i.e., of the great mass of exploited, producers and non-producers, who already find themselves beyond the area of guaranteed wages, or who will in the near future.

The proposal of a kind of intervention based on affinity groups and their coordination and aimed at creating the best conditions for mass insurrection often comes up against a brick wall even amongst the comrades who are interested in it. Many consider it to be out of date, valid at the end of the last century but decidedly out of fashion today. And that would be the case had the conditions of production, in particular the structure of the factory, stayed as they were 150 years ago. The insurrectionary project would undoubtedly be inappropriate were such structures and their corresponding organizations for trade union resistance still in existence. But these no longer exist, and the mentality that went with them has also disappeared. This mentality could be summed up by respect for one's job, taking pride in one's work, having a career. This, along with the sense of belonging to a producer's group in which to associate and resist and form trade union links which could even become the means for addressing more problematic forms of struggle such as sabotage, anti-fascist activity and so on, are all things of the past.

All these conditions have disappeared for good. Everything has changed radically. What we could call the factory mentality has ceased to exist.

The trade union has become a gymnasium for careerists and politicians. Wage bargaining has become a filter for facilitating the adaptation of the cost of labor to the new structures of Capital. Disintegration is extending rapidly beyond the factory to the whole social fabric, breaking bonds of solidarity and all significant human relationships, turning people into face-less strangers, automata immersed in the unlivable confusion of the big cities or in the deathly silence of the provinces. Real interests have been substituted by virtual images created for the purpose of guaranteeing the minimum cohesion necessary to hold the social mechanism as a whole together. Television, sport, concerts, art, and cultural activities constitute a network for those who passively wait for things to happen, such as the next riot, the next crisis, the next civil war, or whatever.

This is the situation we need to bear in mind when talking of insurrection. We insurrectionary and revolutionary anarchists are not referring to something that is still to come about, but to something that is already happening. We are not referring to a remote, far off model, which, like dreamers, we are trying to bring back to life, unaware of the massive transformations that are taking place at the present moment. We live in our time. We are the children of the end of the millennium, actors taking part in the radical transformation of the society we see before us.

Not only do we consider insurrectionary struggle to be possible but, faced with the complete disintegration of traditional forms of resistance, we think that it is the condition towards which we should be moving if we do not want to end up accepting the terms imposed by the enemy and becoming lobotomized slaves, insignificant pawns of the mechanisms of the information technology that will be our master in the near future.

Wider and wider strata of the *excluded* are moving away from the status quo, and consequently from accepting reality or having any hope of a better future. Social strata who once considered themselves to be stable and not at risk are now living in a precariousness they will never be able to escape from by dedication to work and moderation in consumerism.

REVOLUTIONARY ANARCHIST
INSURRECTIONARY ORGANIZATION

We believe that instead of federations and groups organized in the traditional sense—part of the economic and social structures of a reality that no longer exists—we should be forming affinity groups based on the strength of mutual personal knowledge. These groups should be capable of carrying out specific coordinated actions against the enemy.

As far as the practical aspects are concerned, we imagine there would be collaboration between groups and individuals to find the means, documentation and everything else necessary for carrying out such actions. As far as analyses are concerned, we are attempting to circulate as many as possible in our publications and through meetings and debates on specific questions. An insurrectionary organizational structure does not rotate around the central idea of the periodic congress typical of the big syndicalist organizations or the official movement federations. Its points of reference are supplied by the entirety of the situations in the struggle, whether they be attacks on the class enemy or moments of reflection and theoretical inquiry.

Affinity groups could then contribute to the forming of base nuclei. The aim of these structures is to take the place of the old trade unions resistance organizations—including those who insist on the anarcho-syndicalist ideology—in the ambit of intermediate struggles. The base nuclei's field of action would be any situation where class domination enacts a separation between *included* and *excluded*.

Base nuclei are nearly always formed as a consequence of the propulsive actions of insurrectionary anarchists, but they are not composed of anarchists alone. At meetings, anarchists should undertake their task of outlining class objectives to the utmost.

A number of base nuclei could form coordinating structures with the same aim. These specific organizational structures are based on the principles of permanent conflictuality, self-management, and attack.

By permanent conflictuality we mean uninterrupted struggle against class domination and those responsible for bringing it about.

By self-management we mean independence from all parties, trade unions, or patronage, as well as finding the means necessary for organizing and carrying out the struggle on the basis of spontaneous contributions alone.

By attack we mean the refusal of any negotiation, mediation, reconciliation, or compromise with the enemy.

The field of action of affinity groups and base nuclei is that of mass struggles.

These struggles are nearly always intermediary, which means they do not have a direct, immediately destructive effect. They often propose simple objectives, but have the aim of gaining more strength in order to better develop the struggle towards wider objectives.

Nevertheless, the final aim of these intermediate struggles is always attack. However, it is obviously possible for individual comrades or affinity groups to strike at individuals or organizations of Capital and the State independently of any more complex relationship.

Sabotage has become the main weapon of the exploited in their struggle in the scenario we see playing out before our very eyes. Capitalism is creating conditions of control and domination at levels never seen before through information technology which could never be used for anything other than maintaining power.

WHY WE ARE INSURRECTIONARY ANARCHISTS

- Because we are struggling along with the *excluded* to alleviate and ultimately abolish the conditions of exploitation imposed by the *included*.
- Because we consider it possible to contribute to the development of struggles that are appearing spontaneously everywhere, turning them into mass insurrections, that is to say, *actual* revolutions.
- Because we want to destroy the capitalist order of the world which, thanks to computer science restructuring, has become technologically useful to no one but the managers of class domination.
- Because we are for the immediate, destructive attack against the structures, individuals, and organizations of Capital and the State.
- Because we constructively criticize all those who are in

situations of compromise with power in their belief that the revolutionary struggle is impossible at the present time.

- Because rather than wait, we have decided to act, even if the time is not ripe.
- Because we want to put an end to this state of affairs right away, rather than wait until conditions make its transformation possible.

These are the reasons why we are anarchists, revolutionaries, and insurrectionaries.

+++

COMRADES, BEFORE STARTING THIS TALK, A COUPLE OF WORDS in order to get to know each other better. In conferences a barrier is nearly always created between whoever is talking and those who are listening. So, in order to overcome this obstacle we must try to come to some agreement because we are here to do something together, not simply to talk on the one hand and listen on the other. And this common interest needs to be clearer than ever given the questions about to be discussed this evening. Often the complexity of the analyses and the difficulty of the problems that are being tackled separate the person who is talking from those who are listening, pushing many comrades into a passive position. The same thing happens when we read a difficult book which only interests us up to a point, a book with a title such as *Anarchism and Post-industrial Society*, for example. I must confess that if I were to see such a book in a shop window, I'm not sure I'd buy it.

That is why we need to come to some agreement. I think that behind the façade of the problem under discussion, undoubtedly a complex one, the fact that we are anarchists and revolutionary comrades means we should be able to find some common ground. This should permit us to acquire certain analytical instruments with which to better understand reality, and so be able to act upon it more effectively than before. As a revolutionary anarchist I refuse to inhabit two separate worlds:

one of theory and another of practice. As an anarchist revolutionary, my theory is my practice, and my practice my theory.

Such an introduction might not go down well, and it will certainly not please those who support the old theories. But the world has changed. We are faced with a new human condition today, a new and painful reality. This can leave no room for intellectual closure or analytical aristocracies. Action is no longer something that is separate from theory, and this will continue to be the case. That is why it is important to talk about the transformation of capitalism yet again. Because the situation we see before us has already undergone rapid restructuring.

When we find ourselves in a situation like this, we tend to let ourselves be seduced by words. And we all know anarchists' vocation for words. Of course we are for action too. But tonight it is a question of words alone, so we run the risk of getting drunk on them. Revolution, insurrection, destruction, are all words. Sabotage—there, another word. Over the past few days spent here among you I have heard various questions asked. Sometimes they were asked in bad faith, as far as I could tell. But translation from one language to another plays a part in it, and I don't want to be malevolent. I just want to say that it is important not to deceive oneself that my analysis provides the solution to the social problem. I do not believe any of the comrades I have spoken to over the past few days have the solution either. Nor does the anarcho-syndicalist comrade with his analyses based on the centrality of the working class, or the other comrades who as far as I can understand do not seem to agree with him and are proposing an intervention of an insurrectionary nature. No, none of these hypotheses can claim to possess the truth. If anarchism teaches anything it teaches us to be wary of anyone who claims to hold the truth. Anyone who does so, even if they call themselves an anarchist, is always a priest as far as I am concerned. Any discourse must simply aim to formulate a critique of the existent, and if we sometimes get carried away with words, it is the desire to act that gets the better of us. Let us stop here and start thinking again. The destruction of the existent that oppresses us will be a long road. Our analyses are no more than a small contribution so that we can continue our destructive revolutionary activity together in ways that make any small talk simply a waste of time.

So, what can we do? Anarchists have been asking themselves this for a long time: how can we come into contact with the masses? to use a term which often comes up in this kind of discussion, and which I have also heard on various occasions over the past few days. Now, this problem has been faced in two different ways. In the past, throughout the history of anarchism, it has been faced by using the concept of propaganda, that is, by explaining who we are to the masses. This, as we can easily see, is the method used by political parties the world over. Such a method, the use of traditional anarchist propaganda, is difficult today in my opinion, just as the spreading of any other ideology is. It is not so much that people don't want to have anything to do with ideology any longer, but that capitalist restructuring is making it pointless. And I must say here publicly that anarchists are having difficulty in understanding this new reality, and that it is the subject of an ongoing debate within the international anarchist movement. The end of ideology is leading to a situation where traditional anarchist propaganda is becoming pointless. As the effectiveness (or illusion, we do not know which) of propaganda disappears, the path of direct contact with people is opening up. This is a path of concrete struggles, struggles we have already mentioned, everyday questions, but of course one can't exceed one's limitations. Anarchists are a very small minority. It is not by making a lot of noise, or by using advertising techniques that they will be able to make themselves heard by the people. So it is not a question of choosing the most suitable means of communication—because this would take us back to the problem of propaganda, and therefore ideology, again— but rather of choosing the most suitable means of struggle. Many anarchists believe this to be direct attack, obviously within the limits of their possibilities, without imagining themselves to be anyone's gadfly.

I ask you to reflect for a moment on the state of capitalism at the beginning of the 1980s. Capitalism was suffering. It was facing increased labor costs, a restructuring of factories at astronomically high costs, a rigid market, and the possibility of social struggles developing in response to this. And then, think about the conditions six or seven years later. How quickly capitalism changed. It overcame all its difficulties in a way that could never have been predicted, achieving an unprecedented program of economic and imperialist management of the world. Perhaps it does not seem so at the moment, but this program aimed at closing the circle of power is well underway. What has happened? How was a situation so wrought with difficulties able to turn around so quickly and radically?

We all know what happened, it is not the technical side of it that surprises us. Basically, a new technology has been inserted into the productive process. Labor costs have been reduced, productive programs replaced, new forces used in production: we know all this. That is not the aspect of capitalist restructuring that surprises us. No, what astounds us is the latter's ingenious use of the working class. Because this has always formed the main difficulty for capitalism. Capitalist geniality has succeeded in attacking and dismantling the working class, spreading them all over the country, impoverishing, demoralizing, and nullifying them. Of course it was afraid to do this at first. Capital was always afraid to venture along that road, because reductions in the cost of labor have always marked the outbreak of social struggles. But, as its academic representatives had been insisting for some time, the danger no longer exists, or at least it is disappearing. It is now even possible to lay people off, so long as you do it by changing production sectors, so long as others are being prepared to develop an open mentality and are beginning to discuss things. And all the social forces: parties, unions, social workers, the forces of repression, all levels of school, culture, the world of the spectacle, the media, have been rallied to tackle capitalism's new task. This constitutes a worldwide crusade such as has never been seen before, aimed at modeling the new man, the new worker.

What is the main characteristic of this new man? He is not violent, because he is democratic. He discusses things with others, is open to other people's opinions, seeks to associate with others, joins unions, goes on strike (symbolic ones, of course). But what has happened to him? He has lost his identity. He does not know who he really is any longer. He has lost his identity as one of the exploited. Not because exploitation has disappeared, but because he has been presented with a new image of things in which he is made to feel he is a participant. Moreover, he feels a sense of responsibility. And in the name of this social solidarity he is ready to make new sacrifices: adapt, change his job, lose his skills, disqualify himself as a man and a worker. And that is what capitalism has systematically been asking of him over the past ten years, because with the new capitalist restructuring there is no need for qualifications, but simply for a mere aptitude for work, flexibility, and speed. The eye must be faster than the mind, decisions limited and rapid: restricted choices, few buttons to be pressed, maximum speed in execution. Think of the importance that video games have in this project, to give but one example. So we see that worker centrality has disappeared miserably. Capital is capable of separating the *included* from the *excluded*, that is, of distinguishing those who are involved in power from those who will be *excluded* forever. By "power" we mean not only State management, but also the possibility of gaining access to better living conditions.

But what supports this divide? What guarantees the separation? This lies in the different ways that needs are perceived. Because, if you think about it for a moment, under the old-style form of exploitation, exploited and exploiter both desired the same thing. Only the one *had*, and the other did not. If the construction of this divide were to be fully realized, there will be two different kinds of desire, a desire for completely different things. The *excluded* will only desire what they know, what is comprehensible to them and not what belongs to the *included* whose desires and needs they will no longer be able to comprehend because the cultural equipment necessary to do so will have been taken from them for ever.

This is what capitalism is building: an automaton in flesh and bone, constructed in the laboratories of power. Today's world, based on information technology, knows perfectly well that it will never be able to take the machine to the level of man, because no machine will ever be able to do what a man can. So they are lowering man to the level of the machine. They are reducing his capacity to understand, gradually leveling his cultural heritage to the absolute minimum, and creating uniform desires in him.

So when did the technological process we are talking about begin? Did it begin with cybernetics as has been suggested? Anyone who has any experience of such things knows that if poor Norbert Wiener has any responsibility at all, it lies in the fact that he started to play around with robot tortoises. In actual fact, modern technology was born a hundred years ago when an innocent English mathematician started toying with arithmetic and developed binary calculus. Now, following on from that it is possible to identify the various steps in modern technology. But there is one precise moment in which a qualitative leap takes place: when electronics came to be used as the basis upon which the new technology (and consequently the technology for perfecting electronics) was built. And it is impossible to predict how things will evolve, because no one can foresee what the consequences of this entry into a new technological phase will be. We must understand that it is not possible to think in terms of cause and effect. For example, it is naïve to say that the great powers have the atomic potential to blow up the world, even though this is so. This idea, so terrifying and apocalyptic, belongs to the old concept of technology based on the hypothesis of cause and effect: the bombs explode, the world is destroyed. The problem we are talking about here opens up the prospect of a far more dangerous situation because it is no longer a matter of speculation but something that already exists and is developing further. And this development is not based on the principle of cause and effect but on the weaving of unpredictable relations. Just one simple technological discovery, such as a new substance for energy conservation for example, could lead to a series of destructive technological relations which no one in all conscience, no scientist, would be able to predict. It might cause a series of destructive relations which would not only effect the new technologies, but also the old ones, putting the whole world in chaos. This is what is different, and it has nothing to do with cybernetics, which is only the distant relative of the present nightmare.

In light of all this we have been asking ourselves for a long time now: how can we attack the enemy if we do not know it in depth? But, if you think about it, the answer is not all that difficult. We very much enjoy attacking the police, for example, but no one becomes a policeman in order to do so. One informs oneself: how do the police operate? What kind of truncheons do they use? We put together the small amount of knowledge required for us to roughly understand how the police work. In other words, if we decide to attack the police, we simply limit ourselves to obtaining a certain amount of knowledge about them. In the same way, it is not necessary to become engineers in order to attack the new technology, we can simply acquire some basic knowledge, a few practical indications that make it possible for us to attack it. And from this consideration another, far more important one, emerges: that the new technology is not abstract, it is something concrete. For instance, the international communication system is a concrete fact. In order to build abstract images in our heads it needs to spread itself throughout the country. This is the way the new materials are being used, for example in the construction of cables for data transmission. And it is here that it is important to know technology, not how it works in the productive aspect, but how it is spread throughout the country. That is to say, where the directing centers (which are multiple) are to be found and where the communication channels are. These, comrades, are not abstract ideas but physical things, objects that occupy space and guarantee control. It is quite simple to intervene with sabotage in this instance. What is difficult is finding out where the cables are.

We have seen the problem of research and documentation required to attack: at some point this becomes indispensable. At some point, knowledge of technology becomes essential. In our opinion this will be the greatest problem that revolutionaries will have to face over the next few years.

I do not know if any use will be made of the computer in the society of the future, the self-managed society many comrades refer to, just as it is impossible to know whether any use will be made of a considerable number of the new technologies. In fact, it is impossible to know anything about what will happen in this hypothetical society of the future. The only thing I can know, up to a point, concerns the present, and the effects of the use of the new technologies. But we have already gone over this, so there is no point in repeating ourselves. The task of anarchists is to attack, but not on behalf of their own organizational interests or quantitative growth. Anarchists have no social or organizational identity to defend. Their structures are always of an informal character so their attack, when it takes place, is not to defend themselves (or worse still to propagandize themselves), but to destroy an enemy who is striking everyone. And it is in this decision to attack that theory and practice meld together.

An historically unprecedented form of capitalism is appearing on the horizon. When we hear of neoliberalism, this is in fact what is meant. When we hear talk of global domination, this is the project that is being referred to, not the old concept of power, not the old imperialism. It was in the face of this project and its immense capacity to dominate that "real socialism" collapsed. No such thing would ever have happened in the context of the old capitalism. There is no longer any need for the world to be divided into two opposing blocs. The new capitalist imperialism is of an administrative kind. Its project is to manage the world for a small nucleus of *included*, at the cost of the great mass of *excluded*. And with these projects in mind, all possible means are already being used—the new ones we have mentioned, along with the old ones, as old as the world, such as war, repression, barbarity, according to the situation. In this way, in the former Yugoslavia for example, a ferocious war is being waged aimed at reducing a people's capacities as far as possible. Then there will be an intervention in this situation of absolute destruction in the form of a little humanitarian aid which will seem like an enormous amount of help in such conditions of absolute and total misery.

Think of what the state of countries like the former

Yugoslavia would be like without the war. A great powder keg at the gates of western Europe, on our borders, alongside the European Community[3]. A powder keg ready to explode, social contradictions which no economic intervention would ever be able to raise to the level of western consumerism. The only solution was war, the oldest device in the world, and that has been applied. American and world imperialism are intervening in Somalia and Iraq, but there is little doubt that they will intervene in the former Yugoslavia because the probability of rebellion in this area must be reduced to zero. So, old means are being used along with new ones, according to the situation, according to the economic and social context involved.

And one of the oldest weapons in the great arsenal of horrors is racism. On the question of racism and all the misdeeds related to it (neo-nazism, fascism, etc.), let's look for a moment at the differentiated development of capitalist restructuring. In order to understand the problem it is necessary to see how capitalist restructuring cannot solve all its problems just by waving a magic wand. It is faced with many different situations all over the world, each with various levels of social tension. Now, these situations of social tension are making what is lurking in the depths of each one of us rise to the surface, things that we have always put aside, exorcised. Essential factors such as racism, nationalism, the fear of the different, the new, AIDS, the homosexual, are all latent impulses in us. Our cultural superstructure, our revolutionary consciousness, when it puts on its Sunday clothes, obliterates them, hides them all. Then, when we take off our Sunday best, all these things start to reappear. The beast of racism is always present, and capitalism is always ready to use it. In situations such as that which exists in Germany where social tensions have developed rapidly over the past few years, this phenomenon is in constant development. Capital controls racism and uses certain aspects of it, but it is also afraid of it in that the overall management of world power is of a democratic, tolerant, and possibilist nature. From the point of view of utilization, anything (e.g., ideology,

3   The precursor to the European Union. — *Detritus*

fear) can exist—it is all part of Capital's project. We cannot say with certainty that post-industrial capitalism is against racism. We can see a few of its main characteristics, such as its democratic nature, then suddenly discover that in the context of one specific country the same technologically advanced capitalism is using methods that were used a hundred years ago: racism, persecution of Jews, nationalism, attacks on cemeteries, the most hateful and abominable things people can devise. Capital is manifold, its ideology always Machiavellian: it uses both the strength of the lion and the cunning of the fox.

But the main instrument of capitalism the world over are the new technologies. We must think about this a little, comrades, in order to dispel so much confusion. And in doing so we must also consider the possible use of such technology on our part, in changed social conditions, in a post-revolutionary situation. We have already seen how there has been a great qualitative leap from the old technologies to the new—by new technologies we mean those based on computers, lasers, the atom, subatomic particles, new materials, human, animal, and vegetable genetic manipulation. These technologies are quite different from, and have little to do with, the old ones. The latter limited themselves to transforming material, to modifying reality. On the contrary, the new technologies have penetrated reality. They do not simply transform it, they create it, instigating not just molecular changes, possible molecular transformation, but above all creating a mental transformation. Think of the use that is normally made of television. This instrument of communication has got inside us, into our brains. It is modifying our very capacity to see, to understand reality. It is modifying relations in time and space. It is modifying the possibility to step out of ourselves and change reality. In fact, the vast majority of anarchists do not think it possible to make use of this assemblage of modern technologies.

I know that there is an ongoing debate about this. However, this debate is based on a misunderstanding. That is, it is trying to treat two things that are radically different in the same way. The old revolutionary dream, let us say of Spanish anarcho-syndicalism, was that of attacking and defeating power so that the working class could take over the instruments of production and use them in the future society in a way that was more just and free. Now it would be impossible to make a fairer and more free use of these new technologies, because they do not stand passively before us like the old technologies of yesterday, but are dynamic. They move, penetrate deep inside us, have already penetrated us. If we do not hurry to attack, we will no longer be able to understand what we need in order to do so, and rather than us taking the technologies over, it will be the technologies that take us over. It will not be a case of social revolution but of the technological revolution of Capital. This is why a revolutionary use of these new technologies is impossible. The misconception is similar to the old one concerning the possible revolutionary use of war, which many well-known anarchists fell prey to when the First World War broke out. A revolutionary use of war is impossible, because war is always an instrument of death. A revolutionary use of the new technologies is impossible, because the new technologies will always be instruments of death. So all that is left to do is to destroy them—to attack, now, not in the future, not when the project has been completed, not when those who are deceiving themselves stop doing so, but sabotage now, attack now. This is the conclusion we have reached. It is at the moment of the destructive attack that one clarifies what we said to begin with. It is at this point that theory conjoins with practice, and the analysis of post-industrial capitalism becomes an instrument with which to attack capitalism. It becomes an instrument for insurrectionary and revolutionary anarchism in order to direct one's attention to what—the people and the things—makes this project of restructuring of capitalism possible, and whose responsibilities are clear.

Today as never before, striking at the root of inequality means attacking that which makes the unequal distribution of knowledge possible directly. And that is because, for the first time, reality itself is knowledge, for the first time capitalism is knowledge. Whereas the centers where knowledge was elaborated, the universities, for example, were once cloistered places to be consulted at specific times of need, today they are

63   THE INSURRECTIONARY PROJECT

at the center of capitalist restructuring, the center of repressive restructuring. So, a distribution of knowledge is possible. I insist on saying that this is an urgent problem, because it is possible to grasp any difference when one sees it. But when a net separation between two different kinds of knowledge which have no communication between them occurs—the knowledge of the included and that of the excluded—it will be too late. Think of the project of lowering the quality of schooling. Think how mass schooling, once an instrument for gaining knowledge, has been transformed over the past twenty years into an instrument of disqualification. The level of knowledge has been lowered, whereas a restricted minority of privileged continue to acquire other knowledge, in specialized masters degrees organized by Capital.

This, in my opinion, demonstrates the need and urgency for attack yet again. Attack, yes. But not blind attack. Not desperate, illogical attack. Projectual, revolutionary attack, with eyes wide open in order to understand and to act. For example, the situations where Capital exists, and is being realized in time and space, are not all the same. There are some contexts in which insurrection is more advanced than others, yet there is still a great possibility for mass struggles to take place internationally. It is still possible to intervene in intermediate struggles, that is, in struggles that are circumscribed, even locally, with precise objectives that are born from some specific problem. These should not be considered to be of secondary importance. Such kinds of struggle also disturb Capitalism's universal project, and our intervention in them could be considered an element of resistance, putting a brake on the fragmentation of the class structure. I know that many comrades here this evening have experienced such things, and have participated directly in specific struggles.

So, we need to invent new tools. These tools must be capable of affecting the reality of the struggles without the mediation of trade union or party leadership. They must propose clear, even though limited, objectives, ones that are specific, not universal, so in themselves are not revolutionary. We must point to specific objectives because people need to feed their children. We cannot expect everyone to sacrifice themselves in the name of universal anarchism. Limited objectives, then, where our presence as anarchists has the specific task of urging people to struggle directly in their own interests because it is only through direct, autonomous struggle that these objectives can be reached. And once the aim has been reached the nucleus withers and disappears. The comrades then start again, under different conditions.

What comrades are we talking about? What anarchists are we talking about? Many of us are anarchists, but how many of us are available for real, concrete activity? How many of us here today stop short at the threshold of the issue and say: we are present in the struggle, we suggest our project, then the workers, the exploited, do what they like. Our task is done. We have put our conscience at rest. Basically, what is the task of the anarchist if it is not propaganda? As anarchists, we have the solution to all social problems. So we present ourselves to the people who suffer the consequences of the problem, suggest our solution, and go home. No, this kind of anarchism is about to disappear for good. The last remaining mummies belong to history. Comrades must take the responsibility for struggles upon themselves directly and personally because the objective against which the exploited need to struggle in certain situations, and against which they often do not, is a common one because we are exploited just as they are. We are not privileged. We do not live in two different worlds. There is no serious reason as to why they (the so-called masses) should attack before we do. Nor do I see any reason why we should only feel ourselves authorized to attack in their presence. The ideal, certainly, is mass struggle. But in the face of the project of capitalist restructuring anarchists should feel responsible and decide to attack personally, directly, not wait for signs of mass struggle. Because this might never happen. So this is where the destructive act takes place. It is at this point that the circle closes. What are we waiting for?

So, individual acts of destruction too. But here an important objection has been raised: what does one gain by smashing a computer? Does that perhaps solve the problem of technology?

This question, an important one, was presented to us when we worked out the hypothesis of social sabotage. It was said: what result is obtained by destroying an electricity pylon? First of all, the question of sabotage is not aimed so much at the terminal points of technology as at the communications network. So, we are back to the problem of knowledge of the way technology is distributed over the country, and, if you allow me to digress for a moment, I want to point to a serious problem that arises here. I allow myself to use the term "serious problem" because a comparison has been made between what a clandestine armed organization thinks they are doing by striking a specific person, and what, instead, an anarchist insurrectionary structure thinks it is doing by striking a technological apparatus, maintaining that, all said and done, there is not much difference. There is a difference, and it is a very important one. But it is not a question of the difference between people and things. It is an even more important difference, because the aims of the clandestine armed organization contain the error of centrism. By striking the person, the organization believes it is striking the center of Capital. This kind of error is impossible in an anarchist insurrectionary organization, because when it strikes a technological apparatus (or someone responsible for this apparatus), it is fully aware that it is not striking any center of Capitalism.

During the first half of the 1980s, huge mass struggles took place against nuclear power plants in Italy. One of the most important of these was the struggle against the missile base in Comiso. In this context we formed "base nuclei." For three years we struggled alongside the local people. This was a mass struggle, which for various reasons did not succeed in preventing the construction of the base. But that is not the only kind of struggle we consider, it is just one of the possible ones we participate in as insurrectionary anarchists, one of the many intermediary struggles possible.

In another direction, in the years that followed, over 400 attacks took place against structures connected to the electric power supply in Italy. Sabotage against coal-fired electric power stations, the destruction of high-voltage pylons, some of them huge ones that supplied a whole region. Some of these struggles transformed themselves into mass struggles; there was mass intervention in some of the projects of sabotage, in others there was not. On a dark night in the countryside, anonymous comrades would blow up a pylon. These attacks were spread over the whole country, and in my opinion possessed two essential characteristics: they constituted an easily accomplishable attack against Capital, in that they did not use highly destructive technology and, secondly, they are easily copied. Anyone can take a walk in the night. And then, it is also healthy. So anarchists have not passively waited for the masses to awaken, they have considered doing something themselves. In addition to the 400 attacks we know about, one could guess that at least another 400 could have taken place as the State conceals these actions because it is afraid of them. It would be impossible to control a decentralized spread of sabotage all over the country. No army in the world is capable of controlling such activity. As far as I know, not one comrade has been arrested in connection with the known 400 attacks.

I would like to wind up here because I think I have been talking long enough. Our insurrectionary choice is anarchist. As well as being, let us say, a characterological choice, a choice of the heart, it is also a choice of reason, a result of analytical reflection. What we know about global capitalist restructuring today tells us that there is no other way open to anarchists but that of immediate, destructive intervention. That is why we are insurrectionaries and are against all ideology and chatter. That is why we are against any ideology of anarchism, and all chatter about anarchism. The time for pub talk is over. The enemy is right outside this great hall, visible for all to see. It is simply a question of deciding to attack it. I am certain that insurrectionary anarchist comrades will know how to choose the timing and the means for doing so, because with the destruction of this enemy, comrades, it is possible to create anarchy.

What is your identity and that of anarchism?

Today, particularly following the collapse of "actually existing socialism," wide perspectives are opening up for revolutionary anarchism. This should be intended both as an analytical instrument, a means for understanding reality, and as an organizational point of reference for people carrying out social struggles in everyday practice.

What is the position of the Italian anarchist movement in today's society?

The Italian situation is very different from the Greek, partly because Italy has witnessed twenty years of authoritarian revolutionism, i.e., Marxist-Leninist armed groups. The failure of this authoritarian strategy, the aim of which was the conquest of power, has led people to think that all revolutionary struggle is doomed to failure. So anarchists in Italy are faced with a very difficult task today, because on the one hand this problem needs to be clarified, and on the other it is necessary to explain to people what one means by revolutionary struggle, which for anarchists is the destruction of power. And they cannot limit themselves to explaining all this merely in words. It also needs to be done by means of the concrete practice of social struggle, something that is still to happen.

What image do Italian people have of anarchists?

When Italian society has an image of anarchism and anarchists—I say when it has, because often they do not even know what anarchists are—it is either an image that dates back about a hundred years or one supplied by the media. Media images often confuse anarchists, autonomists, and other marginal components of society such as the lumpenproletariat in revolt, even to the point of sometimes calling football hooligans anarchists.

This happens in spite of the fact that the anarchist movement has a long history in Italy?

It is also due to a certain incapacity on the part of anarchists themselves. But it should be said that it is not easy to destroy an opinion that television constructs in a day, in one single program. You must understand that the historical inheritance of the Italian anarchist movement is hardly known, as it is confined to the anarchist minority and academic study. The information that most people receive is limited to the mass media. Due to such conditions, which are the same in Greece, it is not possible to modify the situation from one day to the next, a lot of work is required here.

Is use of the media considered to be part of the insurrectionary project?

This is a very important question, and demonstrates the radical difference between two revolutionary strategies. On the one hand the authoritarian one, that of the old Marxists whose aim was to create spectacular actions—the case which caused the greatest stir being the Moro kidnapping[4]—using the media and, through this instrument of sensationalism, make mass propaganda. According to insurrectionary anarchists this is definitely a losing strategy. Anarchists do not think it is possible to use the media. A limited, subtle dialogue can only be held at a theoretical level, as we are doing now. It cannot exist at a practical level during social struggles, because then, more than at any other time, the media merely carry out the role of supporting the enemy. Insurrectionary anarchists do not believe it is possible for objective, neutral information to exist.

4   Kidnapping of an Italian former prime minister in 1978 by the Marxist-Leninist Red Brigades, resulting in the death of Moro after being held for fifty-four days. — *Detritus*

But are all people prey to the media? Could these means of information not play an important role in making anarchists better known?

I don't believe anything is absolute. In revolutionary activity choices are made that naturally have both positive and negative aspects. When they find themselves in social struggles, insurrectionary anarchists have chosen to refuse this means of communication. Of course that has its price in terms of transmission of the image, but I think that there are more important issues involved such as keeping the media away from the social struggle, although that does not prevent them from carrying out their job of mystification. But here it is a question of revolutionary responsibility, and in Italy more than a few journalists have been attacked personally as a result. So, there is nothing absolute about making such judgements, only practical choices to be made.

It has been argued that Europe is presently moving through a cultural Middle Ages. What is your opinion on this?

This is a complex question, which in order to answer requires at least a couple of words of introduction of a cultural nature. The very concept of a "cultural Middle Ages" shows the limitations of certain information. The Middle Ages is seen negatively, as the "dark ages," which was not the case. The crisis of ideology has also led to a crisis in the idea of progress, upon which the Marxist analysis in particular was based. It is sufficient to think of [György] Lukacs and his theory that reality is proceeding in a determinist and historicist way towards a better future. In the past this ideological concept was also shared by various anarchists, and it was in error. Reality is not moving in a progressive direction, and the conditions of barbarity are always present. There is not one thing in history that can guarantee otherwise. We cannot look at any specific period and say: barbarity is over, fascism is finished with for good. We live with fascism, we can see this better thanks to the crisis in ideology that has opened our eyes a little, but only a little. So, as far as this question is concerned I am of the opinion that we find ourselves, not in the Middle Ages, because the Middle Ages were not barbarian, but in a situation where barbarity is currently possible. So, no, I don't agree with the idea that we are going through a historical period similar to the Middle Ages. We are constantly living in a condition of possible barbarity, but also of possible freedom. It is up to us to choose which road we want to take, and this is the aim of revolutionary activity: understanding which road is the road to freedom, and finding the means to take it.

Concerning the crisis in ideology and the position of [Francis] Fukuyama re: the end of history, the end of ideas—have we reached the end of history or do we have any ideas that are capable of giving us information? And if so, what do we then mean by the concept "the end of history"?

That is a very articulate question. We need to determine what we mean by history. Not by chance is there a relationship between neoliberalism and history, because the old liberalism was historicist, that is, it supported the ideology of history. That kind of history is finished. No matter what the philosophers say, the crisis in the idea of progress concerned a single line proceeding forward through reality and time, necessarily leads to a crisis in the ideology of history, not merely a crisis of history. So, it is not just a matter of a crisis in ideas, because the new liberalism is afraid of a future lack of social control and is circulating the fear of "the end of history" at the level of public opinion. Their aim is to limit people through an ideology of history which, like any ideology, is an instrument of control. So, we have not reached any end historically at all. The fact that we are reaching the end of the millennium just increases the confusion. A neo-millenarianism is being put into circulation for irrational reasons. This is a very dangerous social terrain where we can see a development of all the religious integralisms, including the Christian version, in the name of an abstract need to save humanity. So, it is not a question of "the end of history," but rather of the end of historicism which, like any new ideology of world domination does not know what to do yet. It realizes that it does not yet have the ideally adapted theoretical instruments necessary, whereas academia, i.e. the world—Japanese and American—university has nothing better to do than produce amenities of this kind.

Does history have a cyclical or a linear pattern?

This is also a difficult question. But are all your readers philosophers? I do not know how much deep analysis could be useful, however I will start by establishing that we cannot separate the idea of history from the idea of progress. The idea of progress comes from the revolutionary bourgeoisie who lent themselves to the conquest of power. We need to understand that the idea of progress is an idea of power, of the management of power. Now, the idea of progress requires a linear conception of history, something that was expressed very well by Marx. He thought that the revolutionary clash between the bourgeoisie and the proletariat would necessarily end up with the victory of the proletariat, because the latter were destined to make history. In this he applied the idea of his philosophical mentor, Hegel, who said that the objective idea of the world would make philosophy and would render it useless, so people would no longer need to think. And we have seen how the State did think in place of people in the countries of "actually existing socialism". And these apparently innocent philosophical ideas still lurk amongst small university groups and are discussed by very serious people, savants worried about people's destiny. Then they come out of the universities, move about in reality and contribute to building the concentration camps, determining full-scale massacres, historical tragedies of vast proportions, wars, and genocide.

Now, having established this we can return to the problem of the linear concept of history. What do anarchists put in its place? They suggest inverting Marx's sentiment, that the sleep of reason breeds monsters. On the contrary, anarchists maintain that it is in fact reason that breeds monsters. That is to say the reason of the philosophers, the politicians, the programmers of power, domination, and also of historical ideology. So, as long as it is possible to build States and support exploitation, war and social death, a concept of linear history will be possible. When all that changes, or begins to change, we will finally realize that there is no such thing as linear history but that, according to the intuition of your ancient Greek philosophers (who remain unchallenged today), reality is of a circular movement wherein the barbarity of the past can present itself at any time. In this circular movement nothing is ever old or new, but rather everything is always different—which does not mean that it is more, or less, progressive. That is why it is necessary to begin again each time, identify the enemy, the class enemy, the social enemy, power, and attack it, always with new means. It is something of the work of Sisyphus, and anarchists have this quality of Sisyphus, of always starting at the beginning again, because, like him, they never give up. And with this moral strength of theirs they are superior to the gods, just like Sisyphus.

What do you think of the reappearance of nationalism?

There is not only a reappearance of nationalism, but a reappearance of the most ferocious barbarity of the past. For instance, at least according to what the newspapers report, 20,000 women have been raped in Bosnia. But not in the same way as with all the other armies in the world, because rape is a normal practice of any army, but rather as a deliberate means of fathering Serbians, i.e. as a kind of eugenic program. Such an idea really goes back to the beginning of time and confronts us with tragic considerations. For example, it could be that we (including anarchists) made a mistake concerning man's original goodness and the notion that it was society that made him become bad. We will probably all have to reconsider these concepts. We need to become more intellectually acute, and not be amazed each time these events reoccur in history, and stop placing our hopes in peoples' goodness. Nationalism rises up again because it exists in each one of us, because racism is inside every one of us. The fear of the black man is inside us, in those obscure regions that we are afraid to penetrate, where there is the fear of the different, the foreigner, the AIDS sufferer, the homosexual. These fears exist inside all of us, anarchists included, and we need to talk about them, not hide them under ideology, under great words such as revolution, insurrection, freedom. Because all these beautiful words, if they are developed and brought about in reality by men who are afraid of The Other, run the risk of becoming the instruments of the power of the future, not instruments of liberation.

What do the American ghetto riots such as the one in Los Angeles signify?

The collapse of "actually existing socialism" has brought the apparent universal domination of the Americans to the fore. I say apparent because it is not just the Americans. If we make the mistake, as I seem to see being made during the course of these talks in various towns in Greece over the past few days, of aiming all our criticism at the Americans, we will not be able to understand the general character of the new imperialism. Yes, we have American domination, but also that of the European Community and the Japanese economic colossus. But this triumvirate is different than the power structures of the past. They do not relate to each other in terms of the competition that existed before the collapse of the Soviet empire, but share economic relations of imperialist administration, that is, the construction and maintenance of world domination.

For example, the situation in the former Yugoslavia is only comprehensible through an analysis of the new world imperialism—not only Yankee, but also European. Just think, West Germany has planned to invest thousands of billions of marks over the next ten years to raise East Germany to the level of western consumerism. And that concerns just 17 million people. Now, if such a project were to be made for the whole of the East, from Russia to the former Yugoslavia, an impossible sum would be required. No world power in existence is capable of bringing about such an operation, and world imperialism is aware of this.

What is the solution then? War. That is why there is no American intervention in the former Yugoslavia, because a ferocious, destructive war such as the one now taking place will throw the Serbian, Croatian, and Bosnian people into conditions of such acute poverty that even the slightest intervention, any tiny act of humanitarian aid, will be seen as something positive. Think of such a situation existing without the war. Combative peoples at the gates of Eastern Europe, on the border with Greece. Combative peoples in extreme poverty, with a great capacity for revolutionary social action: what a danger for the European Community! Unfortunately I believe the use of war as an instrument of imperialist management could well be extended, and other examples of this can be seen.

The question of the riots within the American empire is quite different. We must bear in mind that it is not just a question of America, because similar events have also taken place in other countries. More than ten years ago there were riots in Brixton. Then in Switzerland, there was the revolt in Zurich, and in Germany, in Hamburg. Under the conditions of advanced capitalism and precisely due to the process of expulsion of the old proletariat from the factory, there is an increasingly wide strata of new poor who have nothing to lose, and who constitute a threat that is ready to explode at any moment.

It should be said however that the significance of these explosions should not be overestimated. It is true that anarchists have always been in favor of such revolts. Whenever possible, they have participated in them, anywhere—in society or in prison, and always on the side of the weakest. But today they must avoid the theoretical risk of putting the social rebels of the future in the place of the worker-centrism of yesterday. Society is a complex problem, which has nothing in its center. There is not one small part of society that is capable of making the revolution, not even the Los Angeles rioters. Even if we sympathize with them, even if we are alongside them. But we must admit that they are just one element, a sort of involuntary anticipation of possible future mass insurrections, not the main element. And this needs to be said clearly, against all those who deliberately accuse us of forgetting the roles of the other social strata.

What relationship is there between the recent scandals in Italy and Greece, and the new management of power?

The problem of the Italian and Greek scandals is important, and it is no coincidence that these have come to light at the present time, because they correspond to profound changes in the management of power. The new global capitalism, more obvious in some places than others—for example it is more evident in the United States, less so in Greece—needs a political managerial class, not one characterized by ideological agreement, but one technically suited to the managerial needs of global imperialism.

For example, a management of power similar to that of the ex-USSR, or a kind of national socialism, would of necessity have had recourse to mass arrests, mass executions, and would have resolved the problem of a revolt in a few days. A democratic management must use other means. Replacing the head of government is a difficult thing to do, and scandals are an excellent means of achieving the replacement of the old social leadership by the new technocratic one.

Can you tell us anything about Gladio[5] in Italy?

As Machiavelli once wrote, anything is legitimate in the political arena. In Italy the Gladio scandal is the Christian Democrats' response to the denunciation of their clandestine activity after the war, which came to light in the Soviet archives years later. Yes, I said it was the Christian Democrats' response...Contrary to what is believed, it was not the Communist Party that denounced the armed activity of the USA and the Christian Democrats. It was the Christian Democrats themselves who justified their activities in terms of the defense of capitalist

5 Operation Gladio was a NATO/Italian government operation to counter leftist political action, supporting and committing terrorist attacks with the intention of blaming them on leftists. This was part of a general strategy of tension that was Italian government policy throughout the "Years of Lead." — *Detritus*

ideals, in a desperate attempt to save the old political leadership by building a "revolutionary" purity to show that people who had taken up arms in the past should not be made to pay by Capital. Contrary to the logic of other economic scandals, Gladio is an exercise in inverse logic. Whereas the economic scandals are aimed at destroying the old leadership, the Gladio operation tried to save it. Nevertheless this proved impossible, because the needs of world imperialism are greater, and end up by taking over.

In a Greek anarchist paper of 1896 there is an interesting article on ecology. What do you think about the fact that today Capital itself uses ecology as a means of restructuring?

First we need to put this into context, given that you've made reference to a paper from the nineteenth century. Anarchism is not a political movement and never has been. It is a social movement, a carrier of social ideas, and so has always, right from its birth, dealt with the entirety of social problems. If one looks at anarchist papers of the last century, one can find not only the question of ecology addressed but also any other problem that concerns man. The anarchists were the first to talk about free love, eroticism, homosexuality, about all the aspects that concern daily life. This is one of the strengths of anarchism, and has led to the anarchist movement being considered, today as in the past, a great reservoir of ideas into which everyone can dip, and from which Capital itself has derived many concepts. But anarchists are aware of this. They have always put their ideas at the disposal of others, because, as Proudhon said, the worst kind of property is intellectual property. Anarchists have never been afraid that Capital might steal their ideas, because they have always known that they are capable of moving beyond them. So, if at the end of the last century anarchists were ecologists in a particular way, in that they were the only ones to be ecologists, now that Power has "become ecologically-minded" and ecology has become a leading industry, anarchists are no longer ecologists the same as before. They no longer say that it is necessary to save nature, but rather that in order to save nature it is necessary to destroy both those who are polluting it, and those who want to save it using State means.

How do you see yourself?

That is a question that I was asked before many years ago here in Greece, in a very different political situation. The physical conditions were also very different then. At the time I replied: a comrade among comrades. Now that I am older my reply is the same: a comrade among comrades.

FROM RIOT TO INSURRECTION

THERE CAN BE LITTLE DOUBT LEFT ANYWHERE ON THE PLANET that a fundamental change is taking place in the organization of production. This change is most obvious and most felt in the centers of advanced capitalism, but the logic of information technology and decentralized production is now reaching what were once remote peripheral areas, drawing them into an artificial communitarianism whose only real common element is exploitation.

In the "western world" the traditional worker, cornerstone of the authoritarian revolutionary thesis and still a principle element in many anarchist ones, is being tossed out of the grey graveyards of docks, factories and mines, into the coloured graveyards of home-videos, brightly lit job-centers, community centers, multi-ethnic creches, etc., in the muraled ghettos.

As unemployment is coming to be accepted as a perspective of non-employment, capital continues to refine its instruments and direct investment to areas more befitting to its perennial need for expansion. Production of consumer goods is now realised by an intercontinental team of robots, small self-exploiting industries, and domestic labor, in many cases that of children.

The trade unions are at an ebb, and the parties of the left are creeping further to the right as areas for wage claims and social reform are disappearing from the electoral map. What is emerging instead are wide areas of progressive "democratic dissent" in political, social and religious terms: pacifism, ecologism, vegetarianism, mysticism, etc. This "dissenting consensus" sees its most extreme expression in the proposals of "delegitimisation" and "deregulation" by a privileged intellectual strata that reasons exclusively in terms of its own rights.

An ideal society, it might seem, from capital's point of view, with social peace as one of its prime objectives today; or so it would be, this "self-managed" capitalist utopia, were it not for the threat coming from outside the landscaped garden. From the ghetto areas, no longer confined to the Brixton, Toxteth model, but which take many forms: the mining village of the north, the gigantic, gloomy labyrinths of council estates in urban complexes, many of them already no-go areas to police and other forces of repression, and other ever widening areas which until recently housed secure well-paid skilled and white collar workers, are on their way to becoming new ghettos. The ghettos of the future, however, will not necessarily be geographically circumscribed, as the hotbeds of unrest are farmed out to bleak and manageable dimensions, but will be culturally defined, through their lack of means of communication with the rest of capitalist society.

The presence of these ever widening ghettos and the message that is crying out from them is the main flaw in the new capitalist perspective. There are no mediators. There is no space for the reformist politicians of the past, just as there is none for the essentially reformist revolutionaries of the old workerist structures, real or imaginary. The cry is a violent one that asks for nothing. The mini riots or explosions that are now common occurrences, especially in this country, do not have rational demands to make. They are not the means to an end like the bread riots of the past. They have become something in themselves, an irrational thrusting out, often striking easily identifiable targets of repression (police stations, vehicles, schools, government offices, etc.), but not necessarily so. Violence in the football stadiums cannot be excluded from this logic.

Anarchists, since the first major riots—Bristol, Brixton, Toxteth, Broadwater Farm—have seen these events in a positive light, often joining in and contributing a number of extra bricks in the direction of police lines. Anarchist journals exalt these moments of mass insurgence, yet at the same time (the same papers) provide organizational proposals which, if they might have been valid at the beginning of the century or in the 1930s, certainly bear no resemblance to the needs of the present day. The best the most updated ones can offer, using the riots as their point of reference, is to create a specific movement of anarchists with the aim of instilling some revolutionary morality into these patently amoral events. Once again the poverty of our analytical capacity comes to bear.

Up until now, when anarchists have had need of some theoretical content in their publications, they have either resorted to personal opinion, or given a summary of some of the Marxist analyses, critically, but often underlining that there are some points in Marxism that are relevant to anarchist ideas. This gives a "serious" content to a periodical, shows that we are not against theoretical discussions, but leaves the field for anarchist action barren. Without analysis, even at the most basic, rudimentary level, we cannot hope to be in touch with reality. Intuition is not enough. We cannot hope to act, pushing contradictions towards a revolutionary outlet, by simply responding to events as they arise, no matter how violent these events may be.

The Marxist analyses are now nothing but obsolete relics of the dark ages of industrialism. What must be done is to develop our own theses, using as a foundation the wealth of our anarchist methodological heritage. The great strength of anarchism is the fact that it does not rely on one fundamental analysis anchored in time. The living part of anarchism is as alive today as it was four decades ago, or a century ago. What we need to do is to develop instruments that take what is relevant from the past, uniting it with what is required to make it relevant to the present. This can only be done if we have a clear idea of what this reality is. Not what we would like it to be, but what it is, of what is emerging as the real battleground of exploitation today, for battleground it is, even though the dead and wounded have a different aspect to those of yesterday, and the just response of the exploited takes new, less explicit forms. The need to act gets pressing as the ghettos become encapsulated and segregated from the mainstream language and communication of the privileged.

The analysis we are presenting here opens a door in that direction, gives a glimpse of what is happening around and stimulous to develop further investigation and seek to formulate new forms of anarchist intervention that relate to this reality, trying to push it towards our goal of social revolution.

The first text was originally written and presented as the theme of an anarchist conference in Milan in October 1985, held by the comrades of the Italian anarchist bimonthly *Anarchismo*. The second part is a spoken contribution by the same comrade. This explains the concise nature of the text. The author has in fact dedicated many more pages to the insurrectionary thesis, work that he has developed through his active involvement in struggles in Italy over the past two decades.

Jean Weir

FOR AN ANALYSIS OF A PERIOD OF CHANGE.
FROM POST-INDUSTRIAL ILLUSIONS TO POST-REVOLUTIONARY ONES.

CHANGES IN SOCIETY

IN THE EVOLUTION OF SOCIAL CONTRADICTIONS OVER THE PAST few years, certain tendencies have become so pronounced that they can now be considered as real changes.

The structure of domination has shifted from straightforward arbitrary rule to a relationship based on adjustment and compromise. This has led to a considerable increase in demand for services compared to such traditional demands as durable consumer goods. The results have been an increase in those aspects of production based on information technology, the automation of the productive sector, and the preeminence of the services sector (commerce, tourism, transport, credit, insurance, public administration, etc.) over industry and agriculture.

This does not mean that the industrial sector has disappeared or become insignificant; only that it will employ fewer and fewer workers while levels of production remain the same, or even improve. The same is true of agriculture, which will be greatly affected by the process of industrialization, and distinguishable from industry in statistical rather than social terms.

This situation is developing more as a "transition," not

something that is cut and dried, but as a trend. There is no distinct separation between the industrial and post-industrial periods. The phase we are passing through is clearly one of surpassing the obsolete institutions that are being restructured; but it has not yet reached the closure of all factories and the establishment of a reign of computerized production.

The tendency to break up units of production and the demand for small self-exploiting nuclei within a centralized productive project will predominate in the next few years. But within the industrial sector this will be accompanied by such slow adjustments, using traditional means, as are expedient to the cautious strategies of Capital.

This argument relates more to the British and Italian situations which remain far behind their Japanese and American models.

ISLANDS OF LOST MEN

Torn from the factories in a slow and perhaps irreversible process, yesterday's workers are being thrown into a highly competitive atmosphere. The aim is to increase productive capacity, the only consumable product according to the computerized logic of the centers of production. The atomized (and even more deadly) conflicts within Capital itself will extinguish the alternative, revolutionary struggle, with the intention of exacerbating class differences and rendering them unbridgeable.

The most important gains for the inhabitants of the productive "islands," their seemingly greater "freedom," the flexible working hours, the qualitative changes (always within the competitive logic of the market as directed by the order-giving centers) reinforce the belief that they have reached the promised land: the reign of happiness and well-being. Ever increased profits and ever more exacerbated "creativity."

These islands of death are surrounded by ideological and physical barriers, to force those who have no place on them back into a tempestuous sea where no one survives.

So the problem revealing itself is precisely that of the *excluded*.

The *excluded* and the *included*.

The first are those who will remain marginalized. Expelled from the productive process and penalized for their incapacity to insert themselves into the new competitive logic of Capital, they are often not prepared to accept the minimum levels of survival assigned to them by State assistance (increasingly seen as a relic of the past in a situation that tends to extol the virtues of the "self-made man"). These will not just be the social strata condemned to this role through their ethnic origin—today, for example, the West Indians in British society, catalysts of the recent riots in that country—but with the development of the social change we are talking about, social strata which in the past were lulled by secure salaries and now find themselves in a situation of rapid and radical change, will also participate. Even the residual supports that these social strata benefit from (early pensions, unemployment benefits, various kinds of social security, etc.) will not make them accept a situation of growing discrimination. And let us not forget that the degree of consumerism of these expelled social strata cannot be compared to that of the ethnic groups who have never been brought into the sphere of salaried security. This will surely lead to explosions of "social ill-being" of a different kind, and it will be up to revolutionaries to unite these with the more elementary outbreaks of rebellion.

Then there are the included, those who will remain suffocating on the islands of privilege. Here the argument threatens to become more complicated and can only be clearly situated if one is prepared to give credit to man and his real need for freedom. Almost certainly it is the "homecomers" from this sector who will be among the most merciless executants of the attack on Capital in its new form. We are going towards a period of bloody clashes and very harsh repression. Social peace, dreamt of on one side and feared by the other, remains the most inaccessible myth of this new capitalist utopia, heir to the "pacific" logic of liberalism which dusted the drawing room while it butchered in the kitchen, giving welfare at home and massacring in the colonies.

The new opportunities for small, miserable, loathsome daily liberties will be paid for by profound, cruel and systematic discrimination against vast social strata. Sooner or later this will lead to the growth of a consciousness of exploitation inside the privileged strata, which cannot fail to cause rebellions, even if only limited to the best among them. Finally, it should be said that there is no longer a strong ideological support for the new capitalist perspective such as existed in the past, capable of giving support to the exploiters and, more important still, to the intermediate layers of cadres. Wellbeing for the sake of it is not enough, especially for the many groups of people who, in the more or less recent past, have experienced or simply read about liberatory utopias, revolutionary dreams, and attempts, however limited, at insurrectionary projects.

The latter will lose no time in reaching the others. Not all the *included* will live blissfully in the artificial happiness of Capital. Many of them will realize that the misery of one part of society poisons the appearance of wellbeing of the rest, and turns freedom (within the barbed wire fences) into a virtual prison.

STATE PRECAUTIONS

Over the past few years the industrial project has also been modified by the fusion of State controls and methods linked with the political interest in controlling consensus.

Looking at things from the technical side, one can see how the organization of production is being transformed. Production no longer has to take place in one single location, the factory, but is more and more spread over a whole territory, even at considerable distances. This allows industrial projects to develop that take account of a better, more balanced distribution of productive centers within a territory, eradicating some of the aspects of social disorder that have existed in the past such as ghetto areas and industrial super-concentrations, areas of high pollution and systematic destruction of the eco-systems. Capital is now looking forward to an ecological future, opening its arms to the great hodgepodge of environmentalists and becoming a champion of the safeguarding of natural resources, so making the construction of cities of the future with a "human face," socialist or not, seem possible.

The real motivation driving the capitalist project towards distant lands resembling the utopias of yesteryear, is very simple and in no way philanthropic: it is the need to reduce class discontent to a minimum, smoothing the edges off any effective confrontation through a sugarcoated progressive development based on blind faith in the technology of the future.

It is obvious that the most attractive proposals will be made to the *included*, to try as far as possible to avoid defections, which will be the real thorn in the side of tomorrow's capitalists. The individual subjects, if they come from within the sphere of the production process, who turn their goals in a revolutionary direction, will have real weapons to put at the disposal of the revolution against the rule of exploitation.

So far the utopian hope of governing the world through "good" technology has shown itself to be impossible, because it has never taken into account the problem of the physical dimension to be assigned to the ghetto of the *excluded*. They could be recycled into the garden-project in an ungenerous mixture of happiness and sacrifice, but only up to a point.

Tension and repeated explosions of rage will put the fanciful utopia of the exploiters into a very difficult position.

THE END OF IRRATIONAL COMPETITION

It has long been evident. Competition and monopolism were threatening to draw the productive structures into a series of recurrent "crises." Crises of production in most cases. For the old capitalist mentality it was essential to achieve so-called "economies of scale," and this was only possible by working with ever larger volumes of production in order to spread the fixed costs as far as possible. This led to a standardization of production: the accumulation of productive units in particular locations, distributed haphazardly with a colonizing logic (for example the classical Sicilian "cathedrals in the desert": isolated industrial areas, petrol refineries, etc. that were to serve as points of aggregation); the uniformity of products; the division of capital and labor, etc.

The first adjustments to this came about through massive State intervention. The State's presence has opened up various opportunities. It is no longer a passive spectator, simply Capital's "cashier," but has become an active operator, "banker," and entrepreneur.

In essence, these adjustments have meant the diminution of use value, and an increase in the production of exchange value in the interests of maintaining *social peace*.

In bringing to an end its most competitive period, Capital has found a partial solution to its problems. The State has lent a hand with the aim of completely transforming economic production into the production of social peace. This utopian project is clearly unreachable. Sooner or later the machine will shatter.

The new productive process—which has often been defined as *post-industrial*—makes low production costs possible even for small quantities of goods; can obtain considerable modifications in production with only modest capital injections; makes hitherto unseen changes to products possible. This opens up undreamt of horizons of "freedom" to the middle classes, to the productive cadres, and within the golden isolation of the managerial classes. But this is rather like the freedom of the castle for those Teutonic knights of the Nazi kind. Encircled by the mansion walls, armed to the teeth, only the peace of the graveyard reigns within.

None of the makers of the ideologies of post-industrial capitalism have asked themselves what to do about the danger that will come from the other side of the walls.

The riots of the future will become ever more bloody and terrible. Even more so when we know how to transform them into mass insurrections.

CONSCIOUSNESS AND GHETTOIZATION

It will not be unemployment as such to negatively define those to be excluded from the castle of Teutonic knights, but principally the lack of real access to information.

The new model of production will of necessity reduce the availability of information. This is only partly due to the computerization of society. It is one of the basic conditions of the new domination and as such has been developing for at least twenty years, finding its climax in a mass schooling that is already devoid of any concrete operative content.

Just as the coming of machines caused a reduction in the capacity for self-determination during the industrial revolution, marching the mass of workers into factories, destroying peasant culture, and giving Capital a work force who were practically incapable of "understanding" the contents of the new mechanized world that was beginning to loom over them; so now the computer revolution, grafted to the process of adjustment of capitalist contradictions by the State, is about to deliver the factory proletariat into the hands of a new kind of machinery that is armed with a language that will be comprehensible to only a privileged few. The remainder will be chased out and obliged to share the sort of ghetto.

The old knowledge, even that filtered from the intellectuals through the deforming mirror of ideology, will be coded in a machine language and rendered compatible with the new needs. This will be one of the historic occasions for discovering, among other things, the scarcity of real content in the ideological gibberish that has been administered to us over the past two centuries.

Capital will tend to abandon everything not immediately translatable into this new generalized language. Traditional education processes will become devalued and diminish in content, unveiling their real (and selective) substance as merchandise.

In the place of language new canons of behavior will be supplied, formed from fairly precise rules, and mainly developed from the old processes of democratization and assembly, which Capital has learned to control perfectly. This will be doubly useful as it will also give the *excluded* the impression that they are "participating" in public affairs.

The computerized society of tomorrow could even have clean seas and an "almost" perfect safeguarding of the limited resources of the environment, but it will be a jungle of prohi-bitions and rules, of nightmare in the form of deep personal decisions about participating in the common good. Deprived of a language of common reference, the ghettoized will no lon-ger be able to read between the lines of the messages of power, and will end up having no other outlet than spontaneous riot, irrational and destructive, an end in itself.

The collaboration of those members of the *included*, dis-gusted with the artificial freedom of Capital, who become rev-olutionary carriers of an albeit small part of this technology which they have managed to snatch from Capital, will not be enough to build a bridge or supply a language on which to base knowledge and accurate counter-information.

The organized work of future insurrections must solve this problem, must build—perhaps starting from scratch—the basic terms of a communication that is about to be closed off; and which, precisely in the moment of closure, could give life, through spontaneous and uncontrolled reactions, to such man-ifestations of violence as to make past experiences fade into insignificance.

GENERALIZED IMPOVERISHMENT

One should not see the new ghetto as the shanty town of the past, a patchwork of refuse forced on to suffering and depriva-tion. The new ghetto, codified by the rules of the new language, will be the passive beneficiary of the technology of the future. It will also be allowed to possess the rudimentary manual skills required to permit the functioning of objects which, rather than satisfy needs, are in themselves a colossal need.

These skills will be quite sufficient for the impoverished quality of life in the ghetto.

It will even be possible to produce objects of considerable complexity at a reasonable cost, and advertise them with that aura of exclusiveness that traps the purchaser, now a prey to Capital's projects. Moreover, with the new productive con-ditions we will no longer have repetitions of the same objects in series, or change and development in technology only with considerable difficulty and cost. Instead there will be flexible, articulated processes that are interchangeable. It will be possible to put the new forms of control to use at low cost, to influence demand by guiding it and thus create the essential conditions for the production of social peace.

Such apparent simplification of life, both for *included* and *excluded*, such technological "freedom" has led sociologists and economists—as the good people they have always been—to let go and sketch the outlines of an interclassist society capable of living "well" without reawakening the monsters of the class struggle, communism, or anarchy.

The decline of interest in the unions and the removal of any reformist significance they might have had in the past—having become mere transmission belts for the bosses' orders—has come to be seen as the proof of the end of the class struggle and the coming of the post-industrial society. This does not make sense for a variety of reasons that we shall see further on. Trade unionism of any kind has lost its reformist significance, not because the class struggle is over, but because the conditions of the clash have changed profoundly.

Basically, we are faced with the continuation of contradictions which are greater than ever and remain unresolved.

TWO PHASES

To be schematic, two phases can be identified.

In the industrial period capitalist competition and production based on manufacturing, prevailed. The most significant economic sector was the secondary one (manufacturing), which used the energy produced as the transformative resource, and financial capital as the strategic resource. The technology of this period was essentially mechanical and the producer who stood out most was the worker. The methodology used in the projects was empirical, based on experiment, while the organization of the productive process as a whole was based on unlimited growth.

In the post-industrial period that we are approaching, but have not completely entered, the State prevails over capitalist competition and imposes its systems of maintaining consensus and production, with the essential aim of promoting social peace. The elaboration of data and the transformation of services will take the place of the technical mode of manufacturing. The predominant economic sectors become the tertiary (services), the quaternary (specialized finance), the quinary (research, leisure, education, public administration). The main transformative resource is information, which is composed of a complex system of transmission of data, while the strategic resource is provided by the knowledge that is slowly taking the place of financial capital. Technology is abandoning its mechanical component and focusing itself on its intellectual component. The typical element employed by this new technology is no longer the worker but the technician, the professional, the scientist. The method used in the project is based on abstract theory, not experiment as it once was, while the organization of the productive process is based on the coding of theoretical knowledge.

THE SUNSET OF THE WORKER'S LEADING ROLE

Directing our attention to the productive industrial phase, Marxism considered the contribution of the working class to be fundamental to the revolutionary solution of social contradictions. This resulted in the strategies of the workers' movement being greatly conditioned by the objective of conquering power.

Hegelian ambiguity, nourished by Marx, lay at the heart of this reasoning: that the dialectical opposition between proletariat and bourgeoisie could be exacerbated by reinforcing the proletariat indirectly through the reinforcement of Capital and the State. So each victory by repression was seen as the antechamber of the future victory of the proletariat. The whole was set in a progressive vision—typically of the enlightenment—of the possibility of building the "spirit" in a world of matter.

With a few undoubtedly interesting modifications, this old conception of the class struggle still persists today, at least in some of the nightmarish dreams that arise occasionally from the old projects of glory and conquest. A serious analysis has never been made of this purely imaginary conception.

There is only more or less unanimous agreement that workers have been displaced from their central position. First, timidly, in the sense of a move out of the factory into the whole social terrain. Then, more decisively, in the sense of a progressive substitution of the secondary manufacturing sector by the tertiary services sector.

THE SUNSET OF SOME OF THE ANARCHISTS' ILLUSIONS

Anarchists have also had illusions and these have also faded. Strictly speaking, while these illusions were never about the central role of workers, they often saw the world of work as being of fundamental importance, giving precedence to industry over the primary (agricultural) sector. It was anarcho-syndicalism that fueled these illusions.

Even in recent times there has been much enthusiasm for the CNT's rise from the ashes, particularly from those who seem to be the most radical entrepreneurs of the new "roads" of reformist anarchism today.

The main concept of this worker centrality (different from that of the Marxists, but less so than is commonly believed), was the shadow of the Party.

For a long time the anarchist movement has acted as an organization of synthesis, that is, like a party.

Not the whole of the anarchist movement, but certainly its organized forms.

Let us take the Italian FAI (Federazione Anarchica Italiana) for example. To this day it is an organization of synthesis. It is based on a program, its periodical Congresses are the central focus for its activity, and it looks to reality outside from the point of view of a "connecting" center, i.e., as being the synthesis between the reality outside the movement (revolutionary reality), and that within the specific anarchist movement.

Of course, some comrades would object that these remarks are too general, but they cannot deny that the mentality that sustains the relation of synthesis that a specific anarchist organization establishes with the reality outside the movement, is one that is very close to the "party" mentality.

Good intentions are not enough.

Well, this mentality has faded. Not only among younger comrades who want an open and *informal* relationship with the revolutionary movement, but, more important, it has faded in social reality itself.

If industrial conditions of production made the syndicalist struggle reasonable, as it did the Marxist methods and those of the libertarian organizations of synthesis, today, in a post-industrial perspective, in a reality that has changed profoundly, the only possible strategy for anarchists is an informal one. By this we mean groups of comrades who come together with precise objectives, on the basis of affinity, and contribute to creating mass structures that set themselves intermediate aims, while constructing the minimal conditions for transforming situations of simple riot into those of insurrection.

The party of Marxism is dead. That of the anarchists too. When I read criticisms such as those made recently by the social ecologists who speak of the death of anarchism, I realize it is a question of language, as well as of lack of ability to examine problems inside the anarchist movement, a limitation, moreover, that is pointed out by these comrades themselves. What is dead for them—and also for me—is the anarchism that thought it could be the organizational point of reference for the next revolution, that saw itself as a structure of synthesis aimed at generating the multiple forms of human creativity directed at breaking up State structures of consensus and repression. What is dead is the static anarchism of the traditional organizations, based on claiming better conditions, and having quantitative goals. The idea that social revolution is something that must necessarily result from our struggles has proved to be unfounded. It might, then again it might not.

Determinism is dead, and the blind law of cause and effect with it. The revolutionary means we employ, including insurrection, do not necessarily lead to social revolution. The causal model so dear to the positivists of the last century does not in reality exist.

The revolution becomes possible precisely for that reason.

SPEED AND MULTIPLICITY

The reduction of time in data transmission means the acceleration of programmed decision making. If this time is reduced to zero (as happens in electronic "real time"), programmed decisions are not only accelerated but are also transformed. They become something different.

By modifying projects, elements of productive investments are also modified, transferring themselves from traditional capital (mainly financial) to the capital of the future (mainly intellectual).

The management of the different is one of the fundamental elements of reality.

By perfecting the relationship between politics and economy, putting an end to the contradictions produced by competition, by organizing consensus and, more importantly, by programming all this in a perspective of real time, the power structure cuts off a large part of society: the part of the *excluded*.

The greatly increased speed of productive operations will more than anything else give rise to a cultural and linguistic modification. Here lies the greatest danger for the ghettoized.

THE END OF REFORMISM, THE END OF THE PARTY

The party is based on the reformist hypothesis. This requires a community of language, if not of interest. That happened with parties and also with trade unions. Community of language translated itself into a fictitious class opposition that was characterized by a request for improvements on the one hand, and resistance to conceding them on the other.

To ask for something requires a language "in common" with whoever has what we are asking for.

Now the global repressive project is aimed at breaking up this community. Not with the walls of special prisons, ghettoes, satellite cities or big industrial centers; but, on the contrary, by decentralizing production, improving services, applying ecological principles to production, all with the most absolute segregation of the excluded.

And this segregation will be obtained by progressively depriving them of the language that they possessed in common with the rest of society.

There will be nothing left to ask.

THE IGNORANT EXCLUDED

In an era that could still be defined as industrial, consensus was based on the possibility of participating in the benefits of production. In an era where capital's capacity to change is practically infinite, the Capital/State duo will require a language of its own, separate from that of the *excluded* in order to best achieve its new perspective.

The inaccessibility of the dominant language will become a far more effective means of segregation than the traditional confines of the ghetto. The increasing difficulty in attaining the dominant language will gradually make it become absolutely "other." From that moment it will disappear from the desires of the *excluded* and remain ignored by them. From that moment on the *included* will be "other" for the *excluded* and vice versa.

This process of exclusion is essential to the repressive project. Fundamental concepts of the past, such as solidarity, communism, revolution, anarchy, based their validity on the common recognition of the concept of equality. But for the inhabitants of the castle of Teutonic knights the *excluded* will not be men, but simply things, objects to be bought or sold in the same way as the slaves were for our predecessors.

We do not feel equality towards the dog, because it limits itself to barking, it does not "speak" our language. We can be fond of it, but necessarily feel it to be "other," and we do not spare much thought for its kind, at least not at the level of all dogs, preferring to attach ourselves to the dog that provides us with its obedience, affection, or its fierceness towards our enemies.

A similar process will take place in relation to all those who do not share our language. Here we must not confuse language with "tongue." Our progressive and revolutionary tradition has taught us that all men are equal over and above differences of mother tongue. We are speaking here of a possible repressive development that would deprive the *excluded* of the very possibility of communicating with the *included*. By greatly reducing the utility of the written word, and gradually replacing books and newspapers with images, colors and music, for example, the power structure of tomorrow could construct a language aimed at the *excluded* alone. They, in turn, would be able to create different, even creative, means of linguistic reproduction, but always with their own codes and quite cut off from any contact with the code of the *included*, therefore from any possibility of understanding the world of the latter. And it is a short step from incomprehension to disinterest and mental closure.

Reformism is therefore in its death throes. It will no longer be possible to make claims, because no one will know what to ask for from a world that has ceased to interest us or to tell us anything comprehensible.

Cut off from the language of the *included*, the *excluded* will also be cut off from their new technology. Perhaps they will live in a better, more desirable world, with less danger of apocalyptic conflicts, and eventually, less economically caused tension. But there will be an increase in irrational tension.

From the most peripheral areas of the planet, where in spite of "real time" the project of exploitation will always meet obstacles of an ethnic or geographical nature, to the more central areas where class divisions are more rigid, economically based conflict will give way to conflictuality of an irrational nature.

In their projects of control the *included* are aiming at general consensus by reducing the economic difficulties of the *excluded*. They could supply them with a prefabricated language to allow a partial and debilitated use of some of the dominant technology. They could also allow them a better quality of life. But they will not be able to prevent the outbursts of irrational violence that arise from feeling useless, from boredom, and from the deadly atmosphere of the ghetto.

For example in Britain, always a step ahead in the development of Capital's repressive projects, it is already possible to see the beginning of this tendency. The State certainly does not guarantee survival, there is an incredible amount of poverty and unemployment, but the riots that regularly break out there are started by young people—especially West Indian—who know they are definitely cut off from a world that they are already alienated from, from which they can borrow a few objects or ways of doing things, but where they are already beginning to feel "other."

FROM IRRATIONAL RIOT TO CONSCIOUS INSURRECTION

The mass movements that make such an impression on some of our comrades today because of their danger and—in their opinion—uselessness, are signs of the direction that the struggles of tomorrow will take.

Even now many young people are no longer able to evaluate the situation in which they find themselves. Deprived of that minimum of culture that school once provided, bombarded by messages containing aimless gratuitous violence, they are pushed in a thousand ways towards impetuous, irrational, and spontaneous rebellion, and deprived of the "political" objectives that past generations believed they could see with clarity.

The "sites" and expressions of these collective explosions vary a great deal. The occasions also. In each case, however, they can be traced to an intolerance of the society of death managed by the Capital/State partnership.

It is pointless to fear those manifestations because of the traditional ideas we have of revolutionary action within mass movements.

It is not a question of being afraid but of passing to action right away before it is too late.

A great deal of material is now available on techniques of conscious insurrection—to which I myself have made a contribution—from which comrades may realize the superficiality and inconclusiveness of certain preconceived ideas that tend to confuse instead of clarify.

Briefly, we reaffirm that the insurrectionary method can only be applied by informal anarchist organizations. These must be capable of establishing, and participating in the functioning of, base structures (mass organisms) whose clear aim is to attack and destroy the objectives set by power, by applying the principles of self-management, permanent struggle, and direct action.

ANARCHISM & THE INSURRECTIONARY PROJECT
(LECTURE, OCTOBER 13, 1985)

IN ORGANIZING A CONFERENCE LIKE THIS THERE'S A STRANGE contradiction between its formal aspect—such a beautiful hall (though that's a matter of taste), finding ourselves like this, with me up here and so many comrades down there, some I know well, others less so—and the substantial aspect of discussing a problem, or rather a project, that foresees the destruction of all this. It's like someone wanting to do two things at once.

This is the contradiction of life itself. We are obliged to use the instruments of the ruling class for a project that is subversive and destructive. We are facing a real situation that is quite terrible, and in our heads we have a project of dreams.

Anarchists have many projects. They are usually very creative, but at the center of this creativity lies a destructive project that isn't just a dream, a nightmarish dream, but is something based upon, and verified in, the social process around us.

In reality we must presume that this society, cut up and divided by oppositions and contradictions, is moving, if not exactly towards one final destructive explosion, at least towards a series of small destructive eruptions.

In his nightmares this is what the man in the street imagines insurrection to be. People armed, burning cars, buildings destroyed, babies crying, mothers looking for lost children. The great problem is that on this subject the thinking of many anarchists is also not very clear. I have often spoken to comrades about the problems of insurrectionary and revolutionary struggle, and I realize that the same models exist in their minds. What is often visualized are the barricades of the eighteenth century, the Paris Commune, or scenes from the French Revolution.

Certainly, insurrection involves this, but not this alone. The insurrectionary and revolutionary process is this but also something more. We are here today precisely to try to understand this a little better. Let's leave the external aspects of the problem, look one another in the eye, and try thinking about this for a few minutes.

Let us get rid of the idea of insurrection as barricades and instead see in what way the instrument "insurrection" can be observed in reality today, that is, in a reality which is undergoing a rapid and profound transformation.

Today we are not in 1871, nor 1830, nor 1848[1]. Nor are we at the end of the eighteenth century. We are in a situation where industrial production is in transformation, a situation usually described by a phrase, which for convenience we can also use, a "post-industrial" situation.

Some comrades who have reached this analysis, and have thought about the profound changes taking place in the productive situation today, have reached the conclusion that certain old revolutionary models are no longer valid, and that it is necessary to find new ways with which to not only replace these models, but to substantially deny them, and they are proposing new forms of intervention.

Put this way, things seem more logical, fascinating in fact. Why should one endorse a check that expired 100 years ago? Who would ever think that the models of revolutionary intervention of 150 or even 200 years ago, could still be valid? Of

1   Bonanno is here referring to the Paris Commune (1871), and revolutions encompassing western Europe in 1830 and 1848. —*Detritus*

course we are all easily impressed by new roads and new ways of intervening in reality, by creativity and by the new directions that the situation today puts at our disposal. But wait a moment.

We don't intend to use literary quotations here. But someone once said that the capacity of the revolutionary was to grasp as much of the future as possible with what still exists from the past. To combine the knife of our ancestors with the computer of the future. How does this come about?

Not because we are nostalgic for a world where man went to attack his enemy with a knife between his teeth, but quite the contrary, because we consider the revolutionary instruments of the past to be still valid today. Not because of any decision by a minority who takes them up and establishes this validity demagogically without caring what people might think; but because the capacity of the people to find simple means readily at hand, to support any explosion of reaction to repression, represents the traditional strength of every popular uprising.

Let's try to take things in order. There was always something that did not work right with the capitalist project. All those who have ever had anything to do with economic or political analysis have been forced to admit this. Capital's utopia contains something technically mistaken, that is, it wants to do three things that contradict one another: to assure the wellbeing of a minority, exploit the majority to the limits of survival, and prevent insurgence by the latter in the name of their rights.

Throughout the history of capitalism various solutions have been found, but there have been critical moments when Capital has been obliged to find other solutions. The American crisis between the two wars, to give a fairly recent example: a great crisis of capitalist overproduction, a tragic moment linked to other marginal problems that Capital had to face. How did it manage to solve the problem? By entering the phase of mass consumerism, in other words by proposing a project of integration and participation that led—after the experience of the second world war—to an extension of consumerism and thus to an increase in production.

But why did that crisis raise such serious problems for Capital? Because until recently Capital could not bring about production without recourse to massive investment. Let us underline the word "until recently," when Capital had to introduce what are known as economies of scale, and invest considerable amounts of financial capital in order to realize necessary changes in production. If a new type of domestic appliance or a new model of car was required, investment was in the order of hundreds of millions.

This situation confronted Capital with the specter of over-production and with the need to co-opt more and more of the popular strata into massive acquisition. Anyone can see that this could not go on for ever, for sooner or later the game had to end in social violence. In fact the myriad of interventions by Capital and State in their attempts to co-opt turned out to be short lived. Many will remember how ten or fifteen years ago the economists called for economic planning and the possibility of finding work for everyone. That all went up in smoke. The fact is that they were then—note the past tense—moving towards situations of increasing tension. The next stage proposed by Capital was to have State structures intervene in capitalist management, that is, to transform the State from simple armed custodian of Capital's interests into a productive element within capitalism itself. In other words from cashier to banker. In this way, a considerable transformation took place, because the contradictions of economic competition that were beginning to show themselves to be fatal could be overcome by the introduction of consumerism into the strata of the proletariat.

Today we are faced with a different situation, and I ask you to reflect on the importance of this, comrades, because it is precisely the new perspective that is now opening up in the face of repression and Capital's new techniques for maintaining consensus, that makes a new revolutionary project possible.

What has changed? What is it that characterizes post-industrial reality?

What I am about to describe must be understood as a "line of development." It is not a question of Capital suddenly

deciding to engineer a transformation from the decision making centers of the productive process, and doing so in a very
short space of time. Such a project would be fantastic, unreal.
In fact, something like a halfway solution is taking place.

We must bear this in mind when speaking of post-industrial
reality because we don't want—as has already happened—
some comrade to say: wait a moment, I come from the most
backward part of Sicily where still today laborers are taken on
every Sunday by foremen who appear in the piazza offering
them work at 5000 Lire per day[2]. Certainly, this happens, and
worse. But the revolutionary must bear these things in mind
and at the same time be aware of the most advanced points of
reference in the capitalist project. Because, if we were only to
take account of the most backward situations we would not be
revolutionaries, but simply recuperators and reformists capable only of pushing the power structure towards perfecting the
capitalist project.

To return to our theme, what is it that distinguishes post-industrial from industrial reality? Industrial reality was obviously
based on capital, on the concept that at the center of production there was investment, and that that investment had to
be considerable. Today, with new programming techniques, a
change in the aim of capitalist production is quite simple. It is
merely a question of changing computer programs.

Let's examine this question carefully. Two robots in an
industry can take the place of 100 workers. Once, the whole
production line had to be changed in order to alter production.
The 100 workers were not immediately able to grasp the new
productive project. Today the line is modified through one
important element alone. A simple operation in computer programming can change the robots of today into those of tomorrow at low cost. From the productive point of view Capital's
capacity is no longer based on the resources of financial capital,
on investment in other words, but is essentially based on intellectual capital, on the enormous accumulation of productive
capacity that is being created in the field of computer science,

2   About $10 in today's dollars — *Detritus*

the new development in technology that allows such changes to take place.

Capital no longer needs to rely on the traditional worker as an element in carrying out production. This element becomes secondary in that the principal factor in production becomes intellectual capital's capacity for change. So Capital no longer needs to make huge investments or to store considerable stocks in order to regain its initial outlay. It does not need to put pressure on the market and can distribute productive units over wide areas, so avoiding the great industrial centers of the past. It can prevent pollution. We will be able to have clean seas, clean air, better distribution of resources. Think, comrades, reflect on how much of the material that has been supplied to the capitalists by ecologists will be used against us in the future. What a lot of work has been done for the benefit of Capital's future plans. We will probably see industry spread over whole territories without the great centers like Gela, Syracuse, Genoa, Milan, etc. These will cease to exist.

Computer programming in some skyscraper in Milan, for example, will put production into effect in Melbourne, Detroit, or anywhere else. What will this make possible? On the one hand, Capital will be able to create a better world, one that is qualitatively different, a better life. But who for? That is the problem. Certainly not for everybody. If Capital was really capable of achieving this qualitatively better world for everyone, then we could all go home—we would all be supporters of the capitalist ideology. The fact is that it can only be achieved for some, and that this privileged strata will become more restricted in the future than it was in the past. The privileged of the future will find themselves in a similar situation to the Teutonic knights of medieval times, supporting an ideology aimed at founding a minority of "equals"—of "equally" privileged—inside the castle, surrounded by walls and by the poor, who will obviously try continually to get inside.

Now this group of privileged will not just be the big capitalists, but a social strata that extends down to the upper middle classes. A very broad strata, even if it is restricted when compared to the great number of the exploited. However, let's not forget that we are speaking of a project that exists only in tendency.

This strata can be defined as the "included," composed of those who will close themselves inside this castle. Do you think they will surround themselves with walls, barbed wire, armies, guards or police? I don't think so.

Because the prison walls, the ghetto, the dormitory suburb and repression as a whole: police and torture—all of those things that are quite visible today, where comrades and proletarians all over the world continue to die under torture—well, all this could undergo considerable changes in the next few years. It is important to realize that five or ten years today corresponds to 100 years not long ago. The capitalist project is traveling at such speed that it has an exponential progression unequaled to anything that has happened before. The kind of change that took place between the beginning of the 1960s and 1968 takes place in only a few months today.

So what will the privileged try to do? They will try to cut the *excluded* off from the *included*. Cut off in what way? By cutting off communication.

This is a central concept of the repression of the future, a concept which, in my opinion, should be examined as deeply as possible. To *cut off communication* means two things. To construct a *reduced* language that is modest and has an absolutely elementary code to supply to the excluded so that they can use the computer terminals. Something extremely simple that will keep them quiet. And to provide the included, on the other hand, with a language of "the included," so that their world will go towards that utopia of privilege and capital that is sought more or less everywhere. This will be the real wall: the lack of a common language. This will be the real prison wall, one that is not easily scaled.

This problem presents various interesting aspects. Above all there is the situation of the included themselves. Let us not forget that in this world of privilege there will be people who in the past have had extensive revolutionary-ideological experience, and they may not enjoy their situation of privilege tomorrow, feeling themselves asphyxiated inside the Teutonic castle. They will be the first thorn in the side of the capitalist project. The class *homecomers*[3], that is, those who abandon their class. Who were the *homecomers* of the class of yesterday? I, myself, once belonged to the class of the privileged. I abandoned it to become "a comrade among comrades," from privileged of yesterday to revolutionary of today. But what have I brought with me? I have brought my Humanistic culture, my ideological culture. I can only give you words. But the homecomer of tomorrow, the revolutionary who abandons tomorrow's privileged class, will bring technology with him, because one of the characteristics of tomorrow's capitalist project and one of the essential conditions for it to remain standing, will be a distribution of knowledge that is no longer pyramidal but horizontal. Capital will need to distribute knowledge in a more reasonable and equal way—but always within the class of the included. Therefore the deserters of the future will bring with them a considerable number of usable elements from a revolutionary point of view.

And the excluded? Will they continue to keep quiet? In fact, what will they be able to ask for once communication has been cut off? To ask for something, it is necessary to know what to ask for. I cannot have an idea based on suffering and the lack of something of whose existence I know nothing, which means absolutely nothing to me and which does not stimulate my desires. The severing of a common language will make the reformism of yesterday—the piecemeal demand for better conditions and the reduction of repression and exploitation—completely outdated. Reformism was based on the common language that existed between exploited and exploiter. If the languages are different, nothing more can be asked for. Nothing interests me about something I do not understand, which I know nothing about. So, the realization of the capitalist project of the future of this post-industrial project as it is commonly imagined—will essentially be based on keeping the

3   "ritornanti" in the Italian, literally translated as "homecomer" is here used to refer to those who have gained class privilege, but "returned home" to the exploited class in solidarity with others, leaving privilege behind. — *Detritus*

exploited quiet. It will give them a code of behavior based on very simple elements so as to allow them to use the telephone, television, computer terminals, and all the other objects that will satisfy the basic, primary, tertiary, and other needs of the excluded and at the same time ensure that they are kept under control. This will be a painless rather than a bloody procedure. Torture will come to an end. No more bloodstains on the wall. That will stop—up to a certain point, of course. There will be situations where it will continue. But, in general, a cloak of silence will fall over the excluded.

However, there is one flaw in all this. Rebellion in man is not tied to need alone, to being aware of the lack of something and struggling against it. If you think about it this is a concept from the Enlightenment, which was later developed by English philosophical ideology—Bentham and co.—who spoke from a Utilitarian perspective. For the past 150 years our ideological propaganda has been based on these rational foundations, asking why it is that we lack something, and why it is right that we should have something because we are all equal; but, comrades, what they are going to cut along with language is the concept of equality, humanity, fraternity. The included of tomorrow will not feel humanly and fraternally similar to the excluded but will see them as something *other*. The excluded of tomorrow will be outside the Teutonic castle and will not see the included as their possible post revolutionary comrade of tomorrow. They will be two different things. In the same way that today I consider my dog "different" because it does not "speak" to me but barks. Of course I love my dog, I like him, he is useful to me, he guards me, is friendly, wags his tail; but I cannot imagine struggling for equality between the human and the canine races. All that is far beyond my imagination, is *other*. Tragically, this separation of languages could also be possible in the future. And, indeed, what will be supplied to the *excluded*, what will make up that limited code, if not what is already becoming visible: sounds, images, colors. Nothing of that traditional code that was based on the word, on analysis and common language. Bear in mind that this traditional code was the foundation upon which the illuminist and progressive analysis of the transformation of reality was made, an analysis which still today constitutes the basis of revolutionary ideology, whether authoritarian or anarchist (there is no difference as far as the point of departure is concerned). We anarchists are still tied to the progressive concept of being able to bring about change with words. But if Capital cuts out the word, things will be very different. We all have experience of the fact that many young people today do not read at all. They can be reached through music and images (television, cinema, comics). But these techniques, as those more competent than myself could explain, have one notable possibility—in the hands of power—which is to reach the irrational feelings that exist inside all of us. In other words, the value of rationality as a means of persuasion and in developing self-awareness that could lead us to attack the class enemy will decline, I don't say completely, but significantly.

So, on what basis will the excluded act? (Because, of course, they will continue to act). They will act on strong irrational impulses.

Comrades, I urge you to think about certain phenomena that are already happening today, especially in Great Britain, a country which from the capitalist point of view has always been the vanguard and still holds that position today. The phenomena of spontaneous, irrational riots.

At this point we must fully understand the difference between riot and insurrection, something that many comrades do not grasp. A riot is a movement of people which contains strong irrational characteristics. It could start for any reason at all: because someone in the street gets arrested, because the police kill someone in a raid, or even because of a fight between football fans. There is no point in being afraid of this phenomenon. Do you know why we are afraid? Because we are the carriers of the ideology of progress and illuminism. Because we believe the certainties we hold are capable of guaranteeing that we are right, and that these people are irrational—even fascist—provocateurs, people whom it is necessary to keep silent at all costs.

Things are quite different. In the future there will be more and more of these situations of subversive riots that are irrational and unmotivated. I feel fear spreading among comrades in the face of this reality, a desire to go back to methods based on the values of the past and the rational capacity to clarify. But I don't believe it will be possible to carry on using such methods for very long. Certainly we will continue to bring out our papers, our books, our written analyses, but those with the linguistic means to read and understand them will be fewer in number.

What is causing this situation? A series of realities that are potentially insurrectionary or objectively anything but insurrectionary. And what should our task be? To continue arguing with the methods of the past? Or to try moving these spontaneous riot situations in an effectively insurrectionary direction capable of attacking not just the included, who remain within their Teutonic castle, but also the actual mechanism that is cutting out language. In the future we shall have to work towards instruments in a revolutionary and insurrectionary vein that can be read by the excluded.

Let us speak clearly. We cannot accomplish the immense task of building an alternative school capable of supplying rational instruments to people no longer able to use them. We cannot, that is, replace the work that was once done by the opposition when what it required was a common language. Now that the owners and dispensers of the capacity to rationalize have cut communication, we cannot construct an alternative. That would be identical to many illusions of the past. We can simply use the same instruments (images, sounds, etc.) in such a way as to transmit concepts capable of contributing to turning situations of riot into insurrection. This is work that we can do, that we must begin today. This is the way we intend insurrection.

Contrary to what many comrades imagine—that we belong to the eighteenth century and are obsolete—I believe that we are truly capable of establishing this slender air-bridge between the tools of the past and the situations of the future. Certainly it will not be easy to build. The first enemy to be defeated, that within ourselves, comes from our aversion to situations that scare us, attitudes we do not understand, and discourses that are incomprehensible to an old rationalist like myself.

Yet it is necessary to make an effort. Many comrades have called for an attack in the footsteps of the Luddites 150 years ago. Certainly it is always a great thing to attack, but Luddism has seen its day. The Luddites had a common language with those who owned the machines. There was a common language between the owners of the first factories and the proletariat who refused and resisted inside them. One side ate and the other did not, but apart from this by no means negligible difference, they had a common language. Reality today is tragically different. And it will become increasingly different in the future. It will therefore be necessary to develop conditions so that these riots do not find themselves unprepared. Because, comrades, let us be clear about this, it is not true that we can only prepare ourselves psychologically; go through spiritual exercises, then present ourselves in real situations with our flags. That is impossible. The proletariat, or whatever you want to call them, the excluded who are rioting, will push us away as peculiar and suspect external visitors. Suspicious. What on earth can we have in common with those acting anonymously against the absolute uselessness of their own lives and not because of need and scarcity? With those who react even though they have color TV at home, video, telephone, and many other consumer goods; who are able to eat, yet still react? What can we say to them? Perhaps what the synthesis anarchist organizations said in the last century? Malatesta's insurrectionary discourse? This is what is obsolete. That kind of insurrectionary argument is obsolete. We must therefore find a different way, very quickly.

And a different way has first of all to be found within ourselves, through an effort to overcome the old habits inside us and our incapacity to understand the new. Be certain that Power understands this perfectly and is educating the new generations to accept submission through a series of subliminal messages. But this submission is an illusion.

When riots break out we should not be there as *visitors* to a spectacular event, and because in any case, we are anarchists and the event fills us with satisfaction. We must be there as the creators of a project that has been examined and considered in detail be forehand.

What can this project be? That of organizing with the excluded, no longer on an ideological basis, no longer through reasoning exclusively based on the old concepts of the class struggle, but on the basis of something immediate and capable of connecting with reality, with different realities. There must be areas in your own situations where tensions are being generated. Contact with these situations, if it continues on an ideological basis, will end up having you pushed out. Contact must be on a different basis, organized but different. This cannot be done by any large organization with its traditionally enlightened or romantic claim to serve as a point of reference and synthesis in a host of different situations; it can only be done by an organization that is agile, flexible, and able to adapt. An *informal organization* of anarchist comrades—a specific organization composed of comrades having an anarchist class consciousness, but who recognize the limits of the old models and propose different, more flexible models instead. They must touch reality, develop a clear analysis and make it known, perhaps using the instruments of the future, not just the instruments of the past. Let us remember that the difference between the instruments of the future and those of the past does not lie in putting a few extra photographs in our papers. It is not simply a matter of giving a different, more humorous or less pedantic edge to our writing, but of truly understanding what the tools of the future are, of studying and going into them, because it is this that will make it possible to construct the insurrectionary tools of the future, to put alongside the knife that our predecessors carried between their teeth. In this way the air-bridge we mentioned earlier can be built.

Informal organization, therefore, that establishes a simple discourse presented without grand objectives, and without claiming, as many do, that every intervention must lead to social revolution, otherwise what sort of anarchists would we be? Be sure comrades, that social revolution is not just around the corner, that the road has many corners, and is very long. Agile interventions, therefore, even with limited objectives, capable of striking in anticipation the same objectives that are established by the excluded. An organization that is capable of being "inside" the reality of the subversive riot at the moment it happens to transform it into an objectively insurrection-ary reality by indicating objectives, means and constructive conclusions. This is the insurrectionary task. Other roads are impassable today.

Certainly, it is still possible to go along the road of the syn-thesis organization, of propaganda, anarchist education and debate—as we are doing just now of course—because, as we said, this is a question of a project in tendency, of attempting to understand something about a capitalist project that is in development. But, as anarchist revolutionaries, we are obliged to bear this line of development in mind, and prepare ourselves from this moment on to transform irrational situations of riot into an insurrectionary and revolutionary reality.

ARMED JOY

THIS BOOK WAS WRITTEN IN 1977 IN THE MOMENTUM OF THE revolutionary struggles that were taking place in Italy at the time, and that situation, now profoundly different, should be borne in mind when reading it today.

The revolutionary movement, including the anarchist one, was in a developing phase and anything seemed possible, even a generalization of the armed clash.

But it was necessary to protect oneself from the danger of specialization and militarization that a restricted minority of militants intended to impose on the tens of thousands of comrades who were struggling with every possible means against repression and against the State's attempt—rather weak to tell the truth—to reorganize the management of Capital.

That was the situation in Italy, but something similar was also happening in Germany, France, Great Britain, and elsewhere.

In Italy it seemed essential to prevent the many actions carried out against the men and structures of power by comrades every day from being drawn into the planned logic of an armed party such as the Red Brigades.

That is the spirit of this book. To show how a practice of

liberation and destruction can come forth from a joyful logic of struggle, not a mortifying, schematic rigidity within the pre-established canons of a vanguard group.

Some of these problems no longer exist. They have been solved by the hard lessons of history. The collapse of real socialism suddenly reorganized the directing ambitions of the Marxists of every tendency for good. On the other hand, it has not extinguished, but possibly inflamed, the desire for freedom and anarchist communism that is spreading everywhere, especially among the young generations, often without having recourse to the traditional symbols of anarchism—its slogans and theories also being seen with an understandable, but not shareable, gut refusal to be infected with ideology.

This book has become topical again, but in a different way. Not as a critique of a heavy monopolizing structure that no longer exists, but because it can point out the potent capabilities of the individual on his or her road, with joy, to the destruction of all that oppresses and regulates them.

Before ending I should mention that this book was ordered to be destroyed in Italy. The Italian Supreme Court ordered it to be burned. All the libraries that had a copy received a circular from the Home Ministry ordering its incineration. More than one librarian refused to burn the book, considering such a practice to be worthy of the Nazis or the Inquisition, but by law the volume cannot be consulted. For the same reason the book cannot be distributed legally in Italy and many comrades had copies confiscated during the vast wave of raids carried out for that purpose.

I was sentenced to eighteen months of imprisonment for writing this book.

Alfredo M. Bonanno
Catania, July 14, 1993

I

In Paris, 1848, the revolution was a holiday
without a beginning or an end.

—Mikhail Bakunin

WHY ON EARTH DID THESE DEAR CHILDREN SHOOT [INDRO]
Montanelli[1] in the legs? Wouldn't it have been better to have
shot him in the mouth?

Of course it would. But it would also have been a bigger
deal. More vindictive and sombre. To cripple a beast like that
can have a deeper, more meaningful side to it that goes beyond
revenge, beyond punishing him for his responsibility—fascist
journalist and bosses' lackey that he is.

To cripple him forces him to limp, makes him remember.
Moreover, crippling is a more agreeable pastime than shooting
in the mouth with pieces of brain squirting out through the eyes.

The comrade who sets off in the fog every morning and walks
into the stifling atmosphere of the factory, or the office, only to
see the same faces: the foreman, the timekeeper, the spy of the
moment, the Stakhanovite-with-seven-children-to-support,

1   Montanelli was an Italian journalist, supporter of Mussolini,
    though later changed his tune. Following World War II
    Montanelli became a popular conservative writer. Members of the
    Marxist-Leninist guerrilla group *Brigade Rosse* shot Montanelli
    shortly before the writing of this essay.

feels the need for revolution, the struggle and the physical clash, even a mortal one. But he also wants to bring himself some joy now, right away. And he nurtures this joy in his fantasies as he walks along head down in the fog, spends hours on trains or trams, suffocates in the pointless goings on of the office or amidst the useless bolts that serve to hold the useless mechanisms of Capital together.

Remunerated joy, weekends off or annual holidays paid by the boss is like paying to make love. It seems the same but there is something lacking.

Hundreds of theories pile up in books, pamphlets,. and revolutionary papers. We must do this, do that, see things the way this one said or that one said, because they are the true interpreters of the this or that ones of the past, those in capital letters who fill up the stifling volumes of the classics.

Even the need to keep them close at hand is all part of the liturgy. Not to have them would be a bad sign, it would be suspect. It is useful to keep them handy in any case. Being heavy they could always be thrown in the face of some nuisance. Not a new, but nevertheless a healthy confirmation of the validity of the revolutionary texts of the past (and present).

There is never anything about joy in these tomes. The austerity of the cloister has nothing to envy of the atmosphere one breathes in their pages. Their authors, priests of the revolution of revenge and punishment, pass their time weighing up blame and retribution.

Moreover, these vestals in jeans have taken a vow of chastity, so they also expect and impose it. They want to be rewarded for their sacrifice. First they abandoned the comfortable surroundings of their class of origin, then they put their abilities at the disposal of the disinherited. They have grown accustomed to using words that are not their own and to putting up with dirty tablecloths and unmade beds. So, one might listen to them at least.

They dream of orderly revolutions, neatly drawn up principles, anarchy without turbulence. If things take a different turn they start screaming provocation, yelling loud enough for the police to hear them.

Revolutionaries are pious folk. The revolution is not a pious event.

II

I call a cat a cat.

—Nicolas Boileau-Despréaux

We are all concerned with the revolutionary problem of how and what to produce, but nobody points out that production is a revolutionary problem. If production is at the root of capitalist exploitation, to change the mode of production would merely change the mode of exploitation.

A cat, even if you paint it red, is still a cat.

The producer is sacred. Hands off! Sanctify his sacrifice in the name of the revolution, and *les jeux sont faits.*

"And what will we eat?" concerned people will ask. "Bread and string," say the realists, with one eye on the pot and the other on their gun. "Ideas," the muddling idealists state, with one eye on the book of dreams and the other on the human species.

Anyone who touches productivity has had it.

Capitalism and those fighting it sit alongside each other on the producer's corpse, but production must go on.

The critique of political economy is a rationalization of the mode of production with the least effort (by those who enjoy the benefits of it all). Everyone else, those who suffer exploitation, must take care to see that nothing is lacking. Otherwise, how would we live?

The son of darkness sees nothing when he comes out into the light, just like when he was groping around in the dark. Joy blinds him. It kills him. So he says it is a hallucination and condemns it.

The flabby fat bourgeois bask in opulent idleness. So, enjoyment is sinful. That would mean sharing the same sensations as the bourgeoisie and betraying those of the producing proletariat.

Not so. The bourgeois goes to great lengths to keep the process of exploitation going. He is also stressed and never finds time for joy. His cruises are occasions for new investments, his lovers fifth columns for getting information on competitors.

The productivity god also kills its most faithful disciples. Wrench their heads off, nothing but a deluge of rubbish will pour out.

The hungry wretch harbors feelings of revenge when he sees the rich surrounded by their fawning entourage. The enemy must be destroyed before anything else. But save the booty. Wealth must not be destroyed, it must be used. It doesn't matter what it is, what form it takes or what prospects of employment it allows. What counts is grabbing it from whoever is holding on to it at the time so that everyone has access to it.

Everyone? Of course, everyone.

And how will that happen?

With revolutionary violence.

Good answer. But really, what will we do after we have cut off so many heads we are bored with it? What will we do when there are no more landlords to be found even if we go looking for them with lanterns?

Then it will be the reign of the revolution. To each according to their needs, from each according to their ability.

Pay attention, comrade. There is a smell of bookkeeping here. We are talking of consumption and production. Everything is still in the dimension of productivity. Arithmetic makes you feel safe. Two and two make four. Who would dispute this "truth"? Numbers rule the world. If they have done till now, why shouldn't they continue to?

We all need something solid and durable. Stones to build a wall to stem the impulses that start choking us. We all need objectivity. The boss swears by his wallet, the peasant by his spade, the revolutionary by his gun. Let in a glimmer of criticism and the whole scaffolding will collapse.

In its heavy objectivity, the everyday world conditions and reproduces us. We are all children of daily banality. Even when we talk of "serious things" like revolution, our eyes are still glued to the calendar. The boss fears the revolution because it would deprive him of his wealth, the peasant will make it to get a piece of land, the revolutionary to put his theory to the test.

If the problem is seen in these terms, there is no difference between the wallet, land, and revolutionary theory. These objects are all quite imaginary, mere mirrors of human illusion.

Only the struggle is real.

It distinguishes boss from peasant and establishes the link between the latter and the revolutionary.

The forms of organization production takes are ideological vehicles to conceal illusory individual identity. This identity is projected into the illusory economic concept of value. A code establishes its interpretation. The bosses control part of this code, as we see in consumerism. The technology of psychological warfare and total repression also gives its contribution to strengthening the idea that one is human on condition that one produces.

Other parts of the code can be modified. They cannot undergo revolutionary change but are simply adjusted from time to time. Think, for example, of the mass consumerism that has taken the place of the luxury consumerism of years gone by.

Then there are more refined forms such as the self-managed control of production. Another component of the code of exploitation.

And so on. Anyone who decides to organize my life for me can never be my comrade. If they try to justify this with the excuse that someone must "produce" otherwise we will all lose our identity as human beings and be overcome by "wild, savage nature," we reply that the man-nature relationship is a product of the enlightened Marxist bourgeoisie. Why did they want to turn a sword into a pitchfork? Why must man continually strive to distinguish himself from nature?

III

*Men, if they cannot attain what is necessary, tire
themselves with that which is useless.*

—Johann Wolfgang von Goethe

People need many things.

This statement is usually taken to mean that people have
needs which they are obliged to satisfy.

In this way people are transformed from historically determined units into a duality (means and end simultaneously).
They create themselves through the satisfaction of their needs
(i.e. through work) so become the instrument of their own
creation.

Anyone can see how much mythology is concealed in statements such as this. If people distinguish themselves from
nature through work, how can they fulfill themselves in the
satisfaction of their needs? To do this they would already have
become "human," so have fulfilled their needs, which means
they would not have to work.

Commodities have a profoundly symbolic content. They
become a point of reference, a unit of measure, an exchange
value. The spectacle begins. Roles are cast and reproduce
themselves to infinity. The actors continue to play their parts
without any particular modifications.

The satisfaction of needs becomes no more than a reflex,
marginal effect. What matters is the transformation of people into "things" and everything else along with them. Nature
becomes a "thing." Used, it is corrupted, and people's vital
instincts along with it. An abyss gapes open between nature
and people. It must be filled, and the expansion of the commodity market is seeing to it. The spectacle is expanding to the
point of devouring itself along with its contradictions. Stage
and audience enter the same dimension, proposing themselves

for a higher, more far-reaching level of the same spectacle, and so on to infinity.

Anyone who escapes the commodity code does not become objectified and falls "outside" the terrain of the spectacle. They are pointed at. They are surrounded by barbed wire. If they refuse encirclement or an alternative form of codification, they are criminalized. They are clearly mad! It is forbidden to refuse the illusory in a world that has based reality on illusion, concreteness on the unreal.

Capital manages the spectacle according to the laws of accumulation. But nothing can be accumulated forever. Not even capital. A quantitative process in absolute is an illusion, a quantitative illusion to be precise. The bosses understand this perfectly. Exploitation adopts different forms and ideological models precisely to ensure this accumulation in qualitatively different ways, as it cannot continue in the quantitative aspect indefinitely.

The fact that the whole process becomes paradoxical and illusory does not matter much to Capital, because it is precisely that which holds the reins and makes the rules. If it has to sell illusion for reality and that makes money, then let's just carry on without asking too many questions. It is the exploited who foot the bill. So it is up to them to see the trick and worry about recognizing reality. For Capital things are fine as they are, even though they are based on the greatest conjuring trick in the world.

The exploited almost feel nostalgia for this swindle. They have grown accustomed to their chains and become attached to them. Now and then they have fantasies about uprisings and blood baths, then they let themselves be taken in by the speeches of new political leaders. The revolutionary party extends Capital's illusory perspective to horizons it could never reach on its own. The quantitative illusion spreads.

The exploited enlist, count themselves, draw their conclusions. Fierce slogans make bourgeois hearts miss a beat. The greater the number, the more the leaders prance around arrogantly and the more demanding they become. They draw up great programs for the conquest of power. This new power is preparing to spread on the remains of the old. Bonaparte's soul smiles in satisfaction.

Of course, deep changes are being programmed in the code of illusions. But everything must be submitted to the symbol of quantitative accumulation. The demands of the revolution increase as militant forces grow. In the same way, the rate of the social profit that is taking the place of private profit must also grow. So Capital enters a new, illusory, spectacular, phase. Old needs press on insistently under new labels. The productivity god continues to rule, unrivaled.

How good it is to count ourselves. It makes us feel strong. The unions count themselves. The parties count themselves. The bosses count themselves. So do we. Ring-a-round the rosie.

And when we stop counting we try to ensure that things stay as they are. If change cannot be avoided, we will bring it about without disturbing anyone. Ghosts are easily penetrated.

Every now and then politics come to the fore. Capital often invents ingenious solutions. Then social peace hits us. The silence of the graveyard. The illusion spreads to such an extent that the spectacle absorbs nearly all the available forces. Not a sound. Then the defects and monotony of the *mise-en-scène*. The curtain rises on unforeseen situations. The capitalist machinery begins to falter. Revolutionary involvement is rediscovered. It happened in 1968. Everybody's eyes nearly fell out of their sockets. Everyone extremely ferocious. Leaflets everywhere. Mountains of leaflets and pamphlets and papers and books. Old ideological differences lined up like tin soldiers. Even the anarchists rediscovered themselves. And they did so historically, according to the needs of the moment. Everyone was quite dull-witted. The anarchists too. Some people woke up from their spectacular slumber and, looking around for space and air to breathe, seeing anarchists said to themselves, At last! Here's who I want to be with. They soon realized their mistake. Things did not go as they should have in that direction either. There too, stupidity and spectacle. And so they ran away. They closed up in themselves. They fell apart. Accepted Capital's game. And if they didn't accept it they were banished, also by the anarchists.

The machinery of 1968 produced the best civil servants of the new techno-bureaucratic State. But it also produced its antibodies. The process of the quantitative illusion became evident. On the one hand it received fresh lymph to build a new view of the commodity spectacle, on the other there was a flaw.

It has become blatantly obvious that confrontation at the level of production is ineffective. Take over the factories, the fields, the schools, and the neighborhoods and self-manage them, the old revolutionary anarchists proclaimed. We will destroy power in all its forms, they added. But without getting to the roots of the problem. Although conscious of its gravity and extent, they preferred to ignore it, putting their hopes in the creative spontaneity of the revolution. But in the meantime they wanted to hold on to control of production. Whatever happens, whatever creative forms the revolution might express, we must take over the means of production they insisted. Otherwise the enemy will defeat us at that level. So they began to accept all kinds of compromise. They ended up creating another, even more macabre, spectacle.

And spectacular illusion has its own rules. Anyone who wants to direct it must abide by them. They must know and apply them, swear by them. The first is that production affects everything. If you do not produce you are not a man, the revolution is not for you. Why should we tolerate parasites? Should we go to work in place of them perhaps? Should we see to their livelihood as well as our own? Besides, wouldn't all these people with vague ideas, claiming to do as they please, not turn out to be "objectively" useful to the counterrevolution? Well, in that case better attack them right away. We know who our allies are, who we want to side with. If we want to frighten, then let's do it all together, organized and in perfect order, and may no one put their feet on the table or let their pants down.

Let's organize our specific organizations. Train militants who know the techniques of struggle at the place of production. The producers will make the revolution, we will just be there to make sure they don't do anything silly.

No, that's all wrong. How will we be able to stop them from making mistakes? At the spectacular level of organization there are some who are capable of making far more noise than we are. And they have breath to spare. Struggle at the workplace. Struggle for the defense of jobs. Struggle for production.

When will we break out of the cycle? When will we stop biting our tails?

IV

The deformed man always finds mirrors that make him handsome.

—Marquis de Sade

What madness the love of work is!

With great scenic skill Capital has succeeded in making the exploited love exploitation, the hanged man the rope, and the slave their chains.

This idealization of work has been the death of the revolution until now. The movement of the exploited has been corrupted by the bourgeois morality of production, which is not only foreign to it, but is also contrary to it. It is no accident that the trade unions were the first sector to be corrupted, precisely because of their closer proximity to the management of the spectacle of production.

It is time to oppose the non-work aesthetic to the work ethic.

We must counter the satisfaction of spectacular needs imposed by consumer society with the satisfaction of people's natural needs seen in the light of that primary, essential need: the need for communism.

In this way the quantitative evaluation of needs is overturned. The need for communism transforms all other needs and their pressures on people.

Humanity's poverty, the consequence of exploitation, has been seen as the foundation of future redemption. Christianity and revolutionary movements have walked hand in hand throughout history. We must suffer in order to conquer paradise or to acquire the class consciousness that will take us to the revolution. Without the work ethic the Marxist notion of the "proletariat" would not make sense. But the work ethic is a product of the same bourgeois rationalism that allowed the bourgeoisie to conquer power.

Corporatism resurfaces through the mesh of proletarian internationalism. Everyone struggles within their own sector. At most they contact similar people in other countries, through the unions. The monolithic multinationals are opposed by monolithic international unions. Let's make the revolution but save the machinery, the working tool, that mythical object that reproduces the historical virtue of the bourgeoisie, now in the hands of the proletariat.

The heir to the revolution is destined to become the consumer and main actor of the capitalist spectacle of tomorrow. Idealized at the level of the struggle as the beneficiary of its outcome, the revolutionary class disappears in the idealization of production. When the exploited come to be enclosed within a class, all the elements of the spectacular already exist, just as they do for the class of exploiters.

The only way for the exploited to escape the totalizing project of Capital is through the refusal of work, production, and political economy.

But refusal of work must not be confused with "lack of work" in a society which is based on the latter. The marginalized look for work. They do not find it. They are pushed into ghettos. They are criminalized. Then that all becomes part of the management of the productive spectacle as a whole. Producers and unemployed are equally indispensable to Capital. But the balance is a delicate one. Contradictions explode and produce various kinds of crisis, and it is in this context that revolutionary intervention takes place.

So, the refusal of work, the destruction of work, is an affirmation of the need for non-work. The affirmation that people can reproduce and objectify themselves in non-work through the various solicitations that this stimulates in them. The idea of destroying work is absurd if it is seen from the point of view of the work ethic. But how? So many people are looking for work, so many unemployed, and you talk about destroying work? The Luddite ghost appears and puts all the revolutionaries-who-have-read-all-the-classics to fright. The rigid model of the frontal attack on capitalist forces must not be touched. All the failures and suffering of the past are irrelevant; so is the shame and betrayal. Ahead comrades, better days will come, onwards again!

It would suffice to show what the concept of "free time," a temporary suspension of work, is bogged down in today to scare proletarians back into the stagnant atmosphere of the class organizations (parties, unions, and hangers-on). The spectacle offered by the bureaucratic leisure organizations is deliberately designed to depress even the most fertile imagination. But this is no more than an ideological cover, one of the many instruments of the total war that make up the spectacle as a whole.

The need for communism transforms everything. Through the need for communism the need for non-work moves from the negative aspect (opposition to work) to the positive one: the individual's complete availability to themselves, the possibility to express themselves absolutely freely, breaking away from all models, even those considered to be fundamental and indispensable such as those of production.

But revolutionaries are dutiful people and are afraid to break with all models, not least that of revolution, which constitutes an obstacle to the full realization of what the concept means. They are afraid they might find themselves without a role in life. Have you ever met a revolutionary without a revolutionary project? A project that is well defined and presented clearly to the masses? What kind of revolutionary would one be that claimed to destroy the model, the wrapping, the very foundations of the revolution? By attacking concepts such as quantification, class, project, model, historical task, and other such old stuff, one would run the risk of having nothing to do, of being obliged to act in reality, modestly, like everyone else. Like millions of others who are building the revolution day by day without waiting for signs of a fatal deadline. And to do this you need courage.

With rigid models and little quantitative games you remain within the realm of the unreal, the illusory project of the revolution, an amplification of the spectacle of Capital.

By abolishing the ethic of production you enter revolutionary reality directly.

It is difficult even to talk about such things because it does not make sense to mention them in the pages of a treatise. To reduce these problems to a complete and final analysis would be to miss the point. The best thing would be an informal discussion capable of bringing about the subtle magic of wordplay.

It is a real contradiction to talk of joy seriously.

V

Summer nights are heavy. One sleeps badly in
tiny rooms. It is the Eve of the Guillotine.

—Zo d'Axa

The exploited also find time to play. But their play is not joy. It is a macabre ritual. An awaiting death. A suspension of work in order to lighten the pressure of the violence accumulated during the activity of production. In the illusory world of commodities, play is also an illusion. We imagine we are playing, while all we are really doing is monotonously repeating the roles assigned to us by Capital.

When we become conscious of the process of exploitation the first thing we feel is a sense of revenge, the last is joy. Liberation is seen as setting right a balance that has been upset by the wickedness of capitalism, not as the coming of a world of play to take the place of the world of work.

This is the first phase of the attack on the bosses. The phase of immediate awareness. What strikes us are the chains, the whip, the prison walls, sexual and racial barriers. Everything must come down. So we arm ourselves and strike the adversary to make them pay for their responsibility.

During the night of the guillotine the foundations for a new spectacle are laid. Capital regains strength: first the bosses' heads fall, then those of the revolutionaries.

It is impossible to make the revolution with the guillotine

alone. Revenge is the antechamber of power. Anyone who wants to avenge themselves requires a leader. A leader to take them to victory and restore wounded justice. And whoever cries for vengeance wants to come into possession of what has been taken away from them. Right to the supreme abstraction, the appropriation of surplus value.

The world of the future must be one where everybody works. Fine! So we will have imposed slavery on everyone with the exception of those who make it function and who, precisely for that reason, become the new bosses.

No matter what, the bosses must "pay" for their wrongs. Very well! We will carry the Christian ethic of sin, judgement, and reparation into the revolution. As well as the concepts of "debt" and "payment," clearly of mercantile origins.

That is all part of the spectacle. Even when it is not managed by power directly it can easily be taken over. Role reversal is one of the techniques of drama.

It might be necessary to attack using the arms of revenge and punishment at a certain moment in the class struggle. The movement might not possess any others. So it will be the moment for the guillotine. But revolutionaries must be aware of the limitations of such arms. They should not deceive themselves or others.

Within the paranoid framework of a rationalizing machine such as capitalism the concept of the revolution of revenge can even become part of the spectacle as it continually adapts itself. The movement of production seems to come about thanks to the blessing of economic science, but in reality it is based on the illusory anthropology of the separation of tasks.

There is no joy in work, even if it is self-managed. The revolution cannot be reduced to a simple reorganization of work. Not that alone. There is no joy in sacrifice, death, and revenge. Just as there is no joy in counting oneself. Arithmetic is the negation of joy.

Anyone who desires to live does not produce death. A transitory acceptance of the guillotine leads to its institutionalization. But at the same time, anyone who loves life does not embrace their exploiter. To do so would signify that they are against life in favor of sacrifice, self-punishment, work, and death.

In the graveyard of work centuries of exploitation have accumulated a huge mountain of revenge. The leaders of the revolution sit upon this mountain, impassively. They study the best way to draw profit from it. So the spur of revenge must be addressed against the interests of the new caste in power. Symbols and flags. Slogans and complicated analyses. The ideological apparatus does everything that is necessary.

It is the work ethic that makes this possible. Anyone who delights in work and wants to take over the means of production does not want things to go ahead blindly. They know by experience that the bosses have had a strong organization on their side in order to make exploitation work. They think that just as strong and perfect an organization will make liberation possible. Do everything in your power, productivity must be saved at all costs.

What a swindle! The work ethic is the Christian ethic of sacrifice, the bosses' ethic thanks to which the massacres of history have followed each other with worrying regularity.

These people cannot comprehend that it would be possible to not produce any surplus value, and that one could also refuse to do so. That it is possible to assert one's will to not produce, so struggle against both the bosses' economic structures and the ideological ones that permeate the whole of Western thought.

It is essential to understand that the work ethic is the foundation of the quantitative revolutionary project. Arguments against work would be senseless if they were made by revolutionary organizations with their logic of quantitative growth.

The substitution of the work ethic with the aesthetic of joy would not mean an end to life as so many worried comrades would have it. To the question: "What will we eat?" one could quite simply reply: "What we produce." Only production would no longer be the dimension in which man determines himself, as that would come about in the sphere of play and joy. One could produce as something separate from nature, then join with it as something that is nature itself. So it would be possible to stop producing at any moment, when there is enough. Only joy will be uncontrollable. A force unknown to the civilized larvae that populate our era. A force that will multiply the creative impulse of the revolution a thousandfold.

The social wealth of the communist world is not measured in an accumulation of surplus value, even if it turns out to be managed by a minority that calls itself the party of the proletariat. This situation reproduces power and denies the very essence of anarchy. Communist social wealth comes from the potential for life that comes after the revolution.

Qualitative, not quantitative, accumulation must substitute capitalist accumulation. The revolution of life takes the place of the merely economic revolution, productive potential takes the place of crystallized production, joy takes the place of the spectacle.

The refusal of the spectacular market of capitalist illusions will create another kind of exchange. From fictitious quantitative change to a real qualitative one. Circulation of goods will not base itself on objects and their illusionist reification, but on the meaning that the objects have for life. And this must be a life meaning, not a death meaning. So these objects will be limited to the precise moment in which they are exchanged, and their significance will vary according to the situations in which this takes place.

The same object could have profoundly different "values." It will be personified. Nothing to do with production as we know it now in the dimension of Capital. Exchange itself will have a different meaning when seen through the refusal of unlimited production.

There is no such thing as freed labor. There is no such thing as integrated labor (manual-intellectual). What does exist is the division of labor and the sale of the workforce, i.e. the capitalist world of production. The revolution is the negation of labor and the affirmation of joy. Any attempt to impose the idea of work, "fair work," work without exploitation, "self-managed" work where the exploited are to re-appropriate themselves of the whole of the productive process without exploitation, is a mystification.

The concept of the self-management of production is valid only as a form of struggle against capitalism, in fact it cannot be separated from the idea of the self-management of the struggle. If the struggle is extinguished, self-management becomes nothing other than self-management of one's exploitation. If the struggle is victorious the self-management of production becomes superfluous, because after the revolution the organization of production is superfluous and counterrevolutionary.

VI

So long as you make the throw yourself everything is skill and easy winning; only if you suddenly become the one catching the ball that the eternal playmate throws at you, at your center, with all her strength, in one of those arcs of great divine bridge builders: only then is being able to catch strength, not yours but of a world.

—Rainer Maria Rilke

We all believe we have experienced joy. Each one of us believes we have been happy at least once in our lives.

However, this experience of joy has always been passive. We happen to enjoy ourselves. We cannot "desire" joy just as we cannot oblige joy to present itself when we want it to.

All this separation between ourselves and joy depends on our being "separate" from ourselves, divided in two by the process of exploitation.

We work all the year round to have the "joy" of holidays. When these come round we feel "obliged" to "enjoy" the fact that we are on holiday. A form of torture like any other. The same goes for Sundays. A dreadful day. The rarefaction of the illusion of free time shows us the emptiness of the mercantile spectacle we are living in.

The same empty gaze alights on the half empty glass, the TV screen, the football match, the heroin dose, the cinema screen, traffic jams, neon lights, prefabricated homes that have completed the killing of the landscape.

To seek "joy" in the depths of any of the various "recitals" of the capitalist spectacle would be pure madness. But that is exactly what Capital wants. The experience of free time programmed by our exploiters is lethal. It makes you want to go to work. To apparent life one ends up preferring certain death.

No real joy can reach us from the rational mechanism of capitalist exploitation. Joy does not have fixed rules to catalogue it. Even so, we must be able to desire joy. Otherwise we would be lost.

The search for joy is therefore an act of will, a firm refusal of the fixed conditions of Capital and its values. The first of these refusals is that of work as a value. The search for joy can only come about through the search for play.

So, play means something different to what we are used to considering it to be in the dimension of Capital. Like serene idleness, the play that opposes itself to the responsibilities of life is an artificial, distorted image of what it really is. At the present stage of the struggle and the relative constrictions in the struggle against Capital, play is not a "pastime" but a weapon.

By a strange twist of irony the roles are reversed. If life is something serious death is an illusion, in the sense that so long as we are alive death does not exist. Now, the reign of death, i.e. the reign of Capital, which denies our very existence as human beings and reduces us to "things," seems very serious, methodical and disciplined. But its possessive paroxysm, its ethical rigor, its obsession with "doing" all hide a great illusion: the total emptiness of the commodity spectacle, the uselessness of indefinite accumulation and the absurdity of exploitation. So the great seriousness of the world of work and productivity hides a total lack of seriousness.

On the contrary, the refusal of this stupid world, the pursuit of joy, dreams, utopia in its declared "lack of seriousness," hides the most serious thing in life: the refusal of death.

In the physical confrontation with Capital play can take different forms, even on this side of the fence. Many things can be done "playfully" yet most of the things we do, we do very "seriously" wearing the death mask we have borrowed from Capital.

Play is characterized by a vital impulse that is always new, always in movement. By acting as though we are playing, we charge our action with this impulse. We free ourselves from death. Play makes us feel alive. It gives us the excitement of life. In the other model of acting we do everything as though it were a duty, as though we "had" to do it.

It is in the ever new excitement of play, quite the opposite of the alienation and madness of Capital, that we are able to identify joy.

Here lies the possibility to break with the old world and identify with new aims and other values and needs. Even if joy cannot be considered man's aim, it is undoubtedly the privileged dimension that makes the struggle against Capital different when it is pursued deliberately.

VII

Life is so boring there is nothing to do except
spend all our wages on the latest skirt or shirt.
Brothers and Sisters, what are your real desires?
Sit in the drugstore, look distant, empty, bored,
drinking some tasteless coffee? Or perhaps blow it
up or burn it down.

—The Angry Brigade

The great spectacle of Capital has swallowed us all up to our necks. Actors and spectators in turn. We alternate the roles, either staring open-mouthed at others or making others stare at us. We have alighted the glass coach, even though we know it is only a pumpkin. The fairy godmother's spell has beguiled our critical awareness. Now we must play the game. Until midnight, at least.

Poverty and hunger are still the driving forces of the revolution. But Capital is widening the spectacle. It wants new actors on stage. The greatest spectacle in the world will continue to surprise us. Always more complicated, better and better organized. New clowns are getting ready to mount the rostrum. New species of wild beasts will be tamed.

The supporters of quantity, lovers of arithmetic, will be first on and will be blinded by the limelight, dragging the masses of necessity and the ideologies of redemption along behind them.

But one thing they will not be able to get rid of is their seriousness. The greatest danger they face will be a laugh. In the spectacle of Capital, joy is deadly. Everything is gloomy and funereal, everything is serious and orderly, everything is rational and programmed, precisely because it is all false and illusory.

Beyond the crises, beyond other problems of underdevelopment, beyond poverty and hunger, the last fight that Capital will have to put up, the decisive one, is the fight against boredom.

The revolutionary movement will also have to fight its battles. Not just the traditional ones against Capital but new ones, against itself. Boredom is attacking it from within, is causing it to deteriorate, making it asphyxiating, uninhabitable.

Let us leave those who like the spectacle of capitalism alone. Those who are quite happy to play their parts to the end. These people think that reforms really can change things. But this is more an ideological cover than anything else. They know only too well that changing bits is one of the rules of the system. It is useful to Capital to have things fixed a little at a time.

Then there is the revolutionary movement where there is no lack of those who attack the power of Capital verbally. These people cause a great deal of confusion. They come out with grand statements but no longer impress anyone, least of all Capital which cunningly uses them for the most delicate part of its spectacle. When it needs a soloist it puts one of these performers on stage. The result is pitiful.

The truth is that the spectacular mechanism of commodities must be broken by entering the domain of Capital, its coordinating centers, right to the very nucleus of production. Think what a marvelous explosion of joy, what a great creative leap forward, what an extraordinarily aimless aim.

Only it is difficult to enter the mechanisms of Capital joyfully, with the symbols of life. Armed struggle is often a symbol of death. Not because it serves death to the bosses and their servants, but because it wants to impose the structures of the dominion of death itself. Conceived differently it really would be joy in action, capable of breaking the structural conditions imposed by the commodity spectacle such as the military party, the conquest of power, the vanguard.

This is the other enemy of the revolutionary movement. Incomprehension. Refusal to see the new conditions of the conflict. The insistence on imposing models of the past that have now become part of the commodity spectacle.

Ignorance of the new revolutionary reality is leading to a lack of theoretical and strategic awareness of the revolutionary capacity of the movement itself. And it is not enough to say that there are enemies so close at hand as to make it indispensable to intervene right away without looking at questions of a theoretical nature. All this hides the incapacity to face the new reality of the movement and avoid the mistakes of the past that have serious consequences in the present. And this refusal nourishes all kinds of rationalist political illusions.

Categories such as revenge, leaders, parties, the vanguard, quantitative growth, only mean something in the dimension of this society, and such a meaning favors the perpetuation of power. When you look at things from a revolutionary point of view, i.e. the complete definitive elimination of all power, these categories become meaningless.

By moving into the nowhere of utopia, upsetting the work ethic, turning it into the here and now of joy in realization, we find ourselves within a structure that is far from the historical forms of organization.

This structure changes continually, so escapes crystallization. It is characterized by the self-organization of producers at the workplace, and the self-organization of the struggle against work. Not the taking over of the means of production, but the refusal of production through organizational forms that are constantly changing.

The same is happening with the unemployed and the casual

laborers. Stimulated by boredom and alienation, structures are emerging on the basis of self-organization. The introduction of aims programmed and imposed by an outside organization would kill the movement and consign it to the commodity spectacle.

Most of us are tied to this idea of revolutionary organization. Even anarchists, who refuse authoritarian organization, do not disdain it. On this basis we all accept the idea that the contradictory reality of Capital can be attacked with similar means. We do so because we are convinced that these means are legitimate, emerging as they do from the same field of struggle as Capital. We refuse to admit that not everyone might see things the way we do. Our theory is identical to the practice and strategy of our organizations.

The differences between the authoritarians and ourselves are many, but they all collapse before a common faith in the historical organization. Anarchy will be reached through the work of these organizations (substantial differences only appear in methods of approach). But this faith indicates something very important: the claim of our whole rationalist culture to explain reality in progressive terms. This culture bases itself on the idea that history is irreversible, along with that of the analytical capacity of science. All this makes us see the present as the point where all the efforts of the past meet the culminating point of the struggle against the powers of darkness (capitalist exploitation). Consequently, we are convinced that we are more advanced than our predecessors, capable of elaborating and putting into practice theories and organizational strategies that are the sum of all the experiences of the past.

All those who reject this interpretation automatically find themselves beyond reality, which is by definition history, progress, and science. Whoever refuses such a reality is anti-historical, anti-progressive, and anti-scientific. Sentenced without appeal.

Strengthened by this ideological armor we go out into the streets. Here we run into the reality of a struggle that is structured quite differently from stimuli that do not enter the framework of our analyses. One fine morning during a peaceful demonstration the police start shooting. The structure reacts, comrades shoot too, policemen fall. Anathema! It was a peaceful demonstration. For it to have degenerated into individual guerrilla actions there must have been a provocation. Nothing can go beyond the perfect framework of our ideological organization as it is not just a "part" of reality, but is "all" reality. Anything beyond it is madness and provocation. Supermarkets are destroyed, shops, and food and arms depots are looted, luxury cars are burned. It is an attack on the commodity spectacle in its most conspicuous forms. The new structures are moving in that direction. They take form suddenly, with only the minimum strategic orientation necessary. No frills, no long analytical premises, no complex supporting theories. They attack. Comrades identify with these structures. They reject the organizations that give power, equilibrium, waiting, death. Their action is a critique of the wait-and-see suicidal positions of these organizations. Anathema! There must have been a provocation.

There is a break away from traditional political models which is becoming a critique of the movement itself. Irony becomes a weapon. Not closed within a writer's study, but en masse, in the streets. Not only the bosses' servants but also revolutionary leaders from a far off and recent past are finding themselves in a hard place as a result. The mentality of the small-time boss and leading group is also put in crisis. Anathema! The only legitimate critique is that against the bosses, and it must comply with the rules laid down by the historical tradition of the class struggle. Anyone who strays from the seminary is a provocateur.

People are tired of meetings, the classics, pointless marches, theoretical discussions that split hairs in four, endless distinctions, the monotony and poverty of certain political analyses. They prefer to make love, smoke, listen to music, go for walks, sleep, laugh, play, kill policemen, cripple journalists, kill judges, blow up barracks. Anathema! The struggle is only legitimate when it is comprehensible to the leaders of the revolution. Otherwise, there being a risk that the situation might go beyond their control, there must have been a provocation.

Hurry comrade, shoot the policeman, the judge, the boss. Now, before a new police prevent you.

Hurry to say No, before the new repression convinces you that saying no is pointless, mad, and that you should accept the hospitality of the mental asylum.

Hurry to attack Capital before a new ideology makes it sacred to you.

Hurry to refuse work before some new sophist tells you yet again that "work makes you free."

Hurry to play. Hurry to arm yourself

VIII

There will be no revolution until the Cossacks
descend.

—Ernest Cœurderoy

Play is also enigmatic and contradictory in the logic of Capital, which uses it as part of the commodity spectacle. It acquires an ambiguity that it does not in itself possess. This ambiguity comes from the illusory structure of capitalist production. In this way the game simply becomes a suspension of production, a parenthesis of "peace" in everyday life. So play comes to be programmed and used scenically.

When it is outside the dominion of Capital, play is harmoniously structured by its own creative impulse. It is not linked to this or that performance required by the forces of the world of production but develops autonomously. It is only in this reality that play is cheerful, that it gives joy. It does not "suspend" the unhappiness of the laceration caused by exploitation but realizes it to the full, making it become a participant in the reality of life. In this way it opposes itself to the tricks put into act by the reality of death—even through play—to make the gloominess less gloomy.

The destroyers of the death reality are struggling against the mythical reign of capitalist illusion, a reign which, although it aspires to eternity, rolls in the dust of the contingent. Joy emerges from the play of destructive action, from the recognition of the profound tragedy that this implies and an awareness of the strength of enthusiasm that is capable of slaying the cobwebs of death. It is not a question of opposing horror with horror, tragedy with tragedy, death with death. It is a confrontation between joy and horror, joy and tragedy, joy and death.

To kill a policeman it is not necessary to don the judge's robes hastily cleansed of the blood of previous sentences. Courts and sentences are always part of the spectacle of Capital, even when it is revolutionaries who act them out. When a policeman is killed his responsibility is not weighed on the scales, the fight does not become a question of arithmetic. One is not programming a vision of the relationship between revolutionary movement and exploiters. One is responding at the immediate level to a need that has come to be structured within the revolutionary movement, a need that all the analyses and justifications of this world would never have succeeded in imposing on their own.

This need is the attack on the enemy, the exploiters, and their servants. It matures slowly within the structures of the movement. Only when it comes out into the open does the movement pass from the defensive phase to attack. Analysis and moral justification are upstream at the source, not downstream at the feet of those who come out into the streets, poised to make them stumble. They exist in the centuries of systematic violence that Capital has exercised over the exploited. But they do not necessarily come to light in a form that is complete and ready for use. That would be a further rationalization of intentions, our dream of imposing a model on reality that does not belong to it.

Let's have these Cossacks come down. We do not support the role of reaction, that is not for us. We refuse to accept Capital's ambiguous invitation. Rather than shoot our comrades or each other it is always better to shoot policemen.

There are times in history when science exists in the consciousness of those who are struggling. At such times there is no need for interpreters of truth. It emerges from things as they are. It is the reality of the struggle that produces theory.

The birth of the commodity market marked the formation of Capital, the passage from feudal forms of production to the capitalist one. With the entrance of production into its spectacular phase the commodity form has extended to everything that exists: love, science, feelings, consciousness, etc. The spectacle has widened. The second phase does not, as the Marxists maintain, constitute a corruption of the first. It is a different phase altogether. Capital devours everything, even the revolution. If the latter does not break from the model of production, if it merely claims to impose alternative forms, capitalism will swallow it up within the commodity spectacle.

Only the struggle cannot be swallowed up. Some of its forms, crystallizing in precise organizational entities, can end up being drawn into the spectacle. But when they break away from the deep significance that Capital gives to production this becomes extremely difficult.

In the second phase questions of arithmetic and revenge do not make sense. If they are mentioned, they take on a metaphorical significance.

The illusory game of Capital (the commodity spectacle) must be substituted with the real game of the armed attack against it, for the destruction of the unreal and the spectacle.

IX

Do it yourself.

—'Bricoleur' Manual

It's easy. You can do it yourself. Alone or with a few trusted comrades. Complicated means are not necessary. Not even great technical knowledge.

Capital is vulnerable. All you need is to be decided.

A load of talk has made us obtuse. It is not a question of fear. We aren't afraid, just stupidly full of prefabricated ideas we cannot break free from.

Anyone who is determined to carry out his or her deed is

not necessarily a courageous person. They are simply a person who has clarified their ideas, who has realized that it is pointless to make such an effort to play the part assigned to them by Capital in the performance. Fully aware, they attack with cool determination. And in doing so they realize themselves as human beings. They realize themselves in joy. The reign of death disappears before their eyes. Even if they create destruction and terror for the bosses, in their hearts and in the hearts of the exploited there is joy and calm.

Revolutionary organizations have difficulty understanding this. They impose a model that reproduces the reality of production. The quantitative destiny of the latter prevents them from having any qualitative move to the level of the aesthetic dimension of joy. These organizations also see armed attack in a purely quantitative light. Objectives are decided in terms of a frontal clash.

In that way Capital is able to control any emergency. It can even allow itself the luxury of accepting the contradictions, point out spectacular objectives, exploit the negative effects on producers in order to widen the spectacle. Capital accepts the clash in the quantitative field, because that is where it knows all the answers. It has a monopoly of the rules and produces the solutions itself.

On the contrary, the joy of the revolutionary act is contagious. It spreads like a spot of oil. Play becomes meaningful when it acts on reality. But this meaning is not crystallized in a model that governs it from above. It breaks up into a thousand meanings, all productive and unstable. The internal connections of play work themselves out in the action of attack. But the overall sense survives, the meaning that play has for those who are excluded and want to appropriate themselves of it. Those who decide to play first and those who "observe" the liberatory consequences of the game, are essential to the game itself.

The community of joy is structured in this way. It is a spontaneous way of coming into contact, fundamental for the realization of the most profound meaning of play. Play is a communitarian act. It rarely presents itself as one isolated fact. If it does, it often contains the negative elements of psychological repression, it is not a positive acceptance of play as a creative moment of struggle.

It is the communitarian sense of play that prevents arbitrariness in choice of the significance given to the game itself. In the absence of a communitarian relationship the individual could impose their own rules and meanings that would be incomprehensible to anyone else, simply making play become a temporary suspension of the negative consequences of their individual problems (the problems of work, alienation, exploitation).

In the communitarian agreement, play is enriched by a flux of reciprocal actions. Creativity is greater when it comes from reciprocally verified liberated imaginations. Each new invention, each new possibility can be lived collectively without pre-constituted models and have a vital influence even by simply being a creative moment, even if it encounters a thousand difficulties during realization. A traditional revolutionary organization ends up imposing its technicians. It tends unavoidably towards technocracy. The great importance attached to the mechanical aspect of action condemns it along this road.

A revolutionary structure that seeks the moment of joy in action aimed at destroying power considers the tools used to bring about this destruction just that, means. Those who use these tools must not become slaves to them. Just as those who do not know how to use them must not become slaves to those who do.

The dictatorship of tools is the worst kind of dictatorship.

Revolutionaries' most important weapons are their determination, their conscience, their decision to act, their individuality. Arms themselves are merely tools, and as such should continually be submitted to critical evaluation. It is necessary to develop a critique of arms. Too often we have seen the sanctification of the submachine gun and military efficiency.

Armed struggle does not concern weapons alone. These alone cannot represent the revolutionary dimension. It is dangerous to reduce complex reality to one single thing. In fact, play involves this risk. It could make the living experience become no more than a toy, turning it into something magical and absolute. It is not by chance that the machine gun appears in the symbolism of many revolutionary combatant organizations.

We must go beyond this in order to understand joy as the profound significance of the revolutionary struggle, escaping the illusions and traps of part of the commodity spectacle through mythical and mythicized objects.

Capital makes its final effort when faced with armed struggle. It engages itself on its last frontier It needs the support of public opinion in order to act in a field where it is not too sure of itself. So it unleashes a psychological war using the most refined weapons of modern propaganda.

Basically, the way Capital is physically organized at the present time makes it vulnerable to any revolutionary structure capable of deciding its own timing and means of attack. It is quite aware of this weakness and is taking measures to compensate for it. The police are not enough. Not even the army. It requires constant vigilance by the people themselves. Even the most humble part of the proletariat. So, to do this it must divide the class front. It must spread the myth of the danger of armed organizations among the poor, along with that of the sanctity of the State, morality, the law, and so on.

It indirectly pushes these organizations and their militants into assuming specific roles. Once in this "role," play no longer has any meaning. Everything becomes "serious," so illusory; it enters the domain of the spectacular and becomes a commodity. Joy becomes "mask." The individual becomes anonymous, lives out their role, no longer able to distinguish between appearance and reality.

In order to break out of the magic circle of the theatricals of commodities we must refuse all roles, including that of the "professional" revolutionary.

Armed struggle must not let itself become something professional, precisely that division of tasks that the external aspect of capitalist production wants to impose upon it.

"Do it yourself." Don't break up the global aspect of play by reducing it to roles. Defend your right to enjoy life. Obstruct Capital's death project. The latter can only enter the world of creativity and play by transforming who is playing into a "player" the living creator into a dead person who cheats themselves into believing they are alive.

There would be no sense in talking about play any longer if the "world of play" were to become centralized. We must foresee this possibility of Capital taking up the revolutionary proposal again when we put forward our argument of "armed joy." And one way this could come about is through the management of the world of play from the outside. By establishing the roles of the players and the mythology of the toy.

In breaking the bonds of centralization (the military party) one obtains the result of confusing Capital's ideas, tuned as they are into the code of the spectacular productivity of the quantitative market. Action coordinated by joy is an enigma to Capital. It is nothing. Something with no precise aim, devoid of reality. And this is so because the essence, the aims and reality of Capital are illusory, while the essence, aims and reality of revolution are concrete.

The code of the need for communism takes the place of the code of the need to produce. In the light of this need in the community of play, the decisions of the individual become meaningful. The unreal illusory character of the death models of the past is discovered.

The destruction of the bosses means the destruction of commodities, and the destruction of commodities means the destruction of the bosses.

X

The owl takes flight.

—Athenian proverb

May actions that start off badly come to a good end. May the revolution, put off by revolutionaries for so long, be realized in spite of the latter's residual desire for social peace.

Capital will give the last word to the white coats. Prisons will not last for long. Fortresses of a past that survives only in the fantasies of some exalted old reactionary, they will disappear along with the ideology based on social orthopedics. There will no longer be convicts. The criminalization Capital creates will be rationalized, it will be processed through asylums.

When the whole of reality is spectacular, to refuse the spectacle means to be outside reality. Anyone who refuses the code of commodities is mad. Refusal to bow down before the commodity god will result in one's being committed to a mental asylum.

There the treatment will be radical. No more inquisitorial-style torture or blood on the walls, such things upset public opinion. They cause the self-righteous to intervene, give rise to justification and making amends, and disturb the harmony of the spectacle. The total annihilation of the personality, considered to be the only radical cure for sick minds, does not upset anyone. As long as the man in the street feels he is surrounded by the imperturbable atmosphere of the capitalist spectacle he will feel safe from the asylum doors ever slamming shut on him. The world of madness will seem to him to be elsewhere, even though there is always an asylum available next to every factory, opposite every school, behind every patch of land, in the middle of every housing estate.

In our critical obtuseness we must take care not to pave the way for the civil servants in white coats.

Capital is programming a code of interpretation to be circulated at mass level. On the basis of this code public opinion will get used to seeing those who attack the bosses' order of things, that is to say revolutionaries, as practically mad. Hence the need to have them put away in mental asylums. Prisons are also rationalizing along the German model. First they will transform themselves into special prisons for revolutionaries, then into model prisons, then into real concentration camps for brain manipulation, and finally, mental asylums.

Capital's behavior is not dictated by the need to defend itself from the struggles of the exploited alone. It is dictated by the logic of the code of commodity production.

For Capital the asylum is a place where the universality of spectacular functioning is interrupted. Prison desperately tries to do this but does not succeed, blocked as it is by its basic ideology of social orthopedics.

On the contrary, the "place" of the asylum does not have a beginning or an end, it has no history, does not have the mutability of the spectacle. It is the place of silence.

The other "place" of silence, the graveyard, has the faculty to speak aloud. Dead men speak. And our dead speak loudly. They can be heavy, very heavy. That is why Capital will try to have fewer and fewer of them. And the number of "guests" in asylums will increase correspondingly. The "homeland of socialism" has much to impart in this field.

The asylum is the perfect therapeutic rationalization of free time, the suspension of work without trauma to the commodity structure. Lack of productivity without denial of it. The madman does not have to work and in not doing so he confirms that work is wisdom, the opposite of madness.

When we say the time is not ripe for an armed attack on the State we are pushing open the doors of the mental asylum for the comrades who are carrying out such attacks; when we say it is not the time for revolution we are tightening the cords of the straightjacket; when we say these actions are objectively a provocation we don the white coats of the torturers.

When the number of opponents was inconsiderable, grapeshot was effective. A dozen dead can be tolerated. Thirty thousand, a hundred thousand, two hundred thousand would mark a turning point in history, a revolutionary point of reference of such blinding luminosity as to disrupt the peaceful harmony of the commodity spectacle. Besides, Capital is more cunning. Drugs have a neutrality that bullets do not possess. They have the alibi of being therapeutic.

May Capital's statute of madness be thrown in its face. Society is one immense mental asylum. May the terms of the counter-positions be overturned.

The neutralization of the individual is a constant practice in Capital's reified totality. The flattening of opinions is a therapeutic process, a death machine. Production cannot take place without this flattening in the spectacular form of capitalism. And if the refusal of all that, the choice of joy in the face of death, is a sign of madness it is time everyone began to understand the trap that lurks beneath it all.

The whole apparatus of the western cultural tradition is a death machine, the negation of reality, a reign of the fictitious that has accumulated every kind of infamy and injustice, exploitation and genocide. If the refusal of this logic is condemned as madness, then we must distinguish between madness and madness.

Joy is arming itself. Its attack is overcoming the commodity hallucination, machinery, vengeance, the leader, the party, quantity. Its struggle is breaking down the logic of profit, the architecture of the market, the programming of life, the last document in the last archive. Its violent explosion is overturning the order of dependency, the nomenclature of positive and negative, the code of the commodity illusion.

But all this must be able to communicate itself. The passage from the world of joy to the world of death is not easy. The codes are out of phase and end up wiping each other out. What is considered illusion in the world of joy is reality in the world of death and vice versa. Physical death, so much a preoccupation in the death world, is less mortifying than what is peddled as life.

Hence Capital's capacity to mystify messages of joy. Even revolutionaries of the quantitative logic are incapable of understanding experiences of joy in depth. Sometimes they hesitantly make insignificant approaches. At other times they let themselves go with condemnation that is not very different to that of Capital.

In the commodity spectacle it is goods that count. The active element of this accumulated mass is work. Nothing can be positive and negative at the same time within the framework of production. It is possible to assert non-work, not the negation of work but its temporary suspension. In the same way it is possible to assert the non-commodity, the personalized object, but only in the context of "free time," i.e. something that is produced as a hobby, in the time lapses conceded by the productive cycle. In this sense it is clear that these concepts, non-work and the non-commodity, are functional to the general model of production.

Only by clarifying the meaning of joy and the corresponding meaning of death as components of two opposing worlds struggling against each other is it possible to communicate elements of the actions of joy. Without illuding ourselves that we can communicate all of them. Anyone who begins to experience joy even in a perspective not directly linked to the attack on Capital is more willing to grasp the significance of the attack, at least more than those who remain tied to an outdated vision of the clash based on the illusion of quantity.

So the owl could still take wing and fly.

XI

Forward everyone! And with arms and heart,
word and pen, dagger and gun, irony and curse,
theft, poisoning and arson, let's make…war on
society!…

—Joseph Déjacque

Let's be done with waiting, doubts, dreams of social peace, little compromises and naivety. All metaphorical rubbish supplied to us in the shops of capitalism. Let's put aside the great analyses that explain everything down to the most minute detail. Huge volumes filled with common sense and fear. Let's put aside democratic and bourgeois illusions of discussion and dialogue, debate and assembly and the enlightened capabilities of the Mafiosi bosses. Let's put aside the wisdom that the bourgeois work ethic has dug into our hearts. Let's put aside the centuries of Christianity that have educated us to sacrifice and obedience. Let's put aside priests, bosses, revolutionary leaders, less revolutionary ones, and those who aren't revolutionary at all. Let's put aside numbers, illusions of quantity, the laws of the market. Let us sit for a moment on the ruins of the history of the persecuted, and reflect.

The world does not belong to us. If it has a master who is stupid enough to want it the way it is, let him have it. Let him count the ruins in the place of buildings, the graveyards in the place of cities, the mud in the place of rivers and the putrid sludge in the place of seas.

The greatest conjuring trick in the world no longer enchants us.

We are certain that communities of joy will emerge from our struggle here and now.

And for the first time life will triumph over death.

LOCKED UP

PRISON HAS COME OUT OF THE SHADOWS INTO THE LIMELIGHT, as not a day passes without some allusion to "solving the problem" of the State's overflowing dungeons. Advances in surveillance technology are offering alternative models of isolation and control that could see a large number of the latters' potentially explosive inmates defused and—opportunely tagged or microchipped—sent back to the urban ghettos of Capital from whence they came. The main obstacle, bolstered by some retrograde attempts to gain votes through a sworn intractability concerning the "enemy within," is power's need for mass consensus from those it had led to believe that the State's protection racket and promise of long custodial sentences were the ultimate social guarantee. The dilemma has given space to a whole range of social cops in an ongoing battle that the sycophantic media have not missed the opportunity to illuminate. The occult world of prison never fails to provide good headlines for those in search of a frisson, "enlightened discussion" or fodder for animated pub talk (the latter often concluding with a call for the reinstatement of the death penalty).

In actual fact, we are witnessing the labor pains of a transitional period concerning the whole question of sanctions and punishment in accordance with the requirements of post-industrial Capital. The reality of enclosure, of being locked up in reinforced strongboxes for days, years, decades on end, is truly in contrast with the prevailing model of social democracy, which would prefer the perfect world of identity and participation also for those who accept the prison condition as their rightful penance.

And so once again, following the feminist issue, the work issue (flexitime, mobility), ecology, etc., we come to the point where the ever-adjusting requirements of power meet the solicitations of the concerned left of the left, obsolete Stalinists and renegade revolutionaries head on. Abolish prison! has become the slogan of the moment, backed up with myriads of tomes, specialist theses on prison conditions and alternative accountancies of crime and retribution worthy of the fathers of the Inquisition.

Separation is the essence of politics, and by isolating prison from the State and Capital as a whole, the harbingers of social surgery can find allies across the whole societal spectrum from priests to social workers, university professors to ex-cons. There is an answer for everything in the fantasy world of alternatives, every bad coin has its flip side. But the totality of prison is not simply a *place*, it is also a condition, the antithesis of which is freedom. By the same token, the absence of freedom is prison and only when we perceive the latter as our own condition, realizing that it is just a question of degree, will we be able to enter the destructive dimension completely, without measure. Only if we combine empathy with projectuality, disgust for the institution and its putrid essence with hatred for the invisible shackles that bind us all, will we be capable of divesting ourselves of the viscid altruism that dams up the free-flowing energy of revolt. Prison is not a domain reserved for "specialists" such as those who have done time themselves or have a particular rapport with individual prisoners, it is the underlying reality of everyday life, each and every discourse of Capital taken to its logical conclusion.

The words that follow were spoken by a comrade in struggle, a struggle where prison has always been present both as a

grim reality and an essential objective in the extensive destruction that "storming the heavens" implies. Little did he know
as he wrote the introduction to the Italian publication of the
transcription from Rebibbia prison in 1997, that a six year
sentence awaited him as the outcome of the infamous Marini
trial. It should not go unsaid that, after being presented for
public crucifixion as head of an inexistent armed gang, three
of these years were for a "crime of opinion," i.e. for the written word, the other three for an unsubstantiated accusation of
involvement in a bank robbery. But that is not what we want
to talk about here. Neither victim nor political prisoner, what
follows are not the prison memoirs of Alfredo Bonanno, but a
contribution by a comrade among comrades, a prisoner among
prisoners, to a struggle that will continue until all prisons are
destroyed and not one stone of them is left standing.

Perhaps the transcription of a meeting between comrades
with its subtle tonal nuances, smiles, intensity and laughter
becomes monochrome and a little difficult to follow in the aus-
tere pages of a pamphlet. The tools of the writer were aside in
favor of the irrepeatable moment, the unique encounter of mind
and spirit that occurs between comrades when they meet and
talk face to face. The discussion meanders from an immediate
clarification that it will contain no vestiges of specialization,
to various anecdotes illustrating some personal recollections
of life behind bars, to underlining precise tendencies in the
evolution of punishment, etc., all linked by one guiding thread:
the impelling need to destroy prisons along with the rest of the
structures of Capital. Nothing less will do. No concession to
the pleasure of immediate gratification granted by success in
single issue reforms. No taking refuge in complicated specialist inquests for the initiated. No negation of the individual in
the name of "subsumption." Prisons are undeniably objective,
material structures, but there are as many of them as there are
prisoners, because like every other moment of life in society,
prison is both a collective and a uniquely individual experience.

One of the main themes of the discourse is the project of
power that is already underway—and would be much more so
were it not for the problem of mass consensus that needs to

be re-educated to accept new repressive trends—of separation between "irreducible" prisoners and the others, the ones that are willing to participate in their own 're-education' and re-insertion into the social marasmus. It is essential to grasp this concept. As science gradually takes over the task of social control from that previously carried out by law, a vast proportion of the prison population will be created as a result of behavioral misdemeanors as opposed to conscious lawbreakers. The latter will tend to become a minority of irreducible "outlaws" who are not prepared to obey the rules of society, be they outside or within the prison walls. The great mass of prisoners will be orientated towards re-insertion through behavior-modifying courses and alternative forms of control using all the paraphernalia on offer by a proliferation of technological gadgets, mobile phones, curfews, etc. For the rest, the intrepid "outlaws" the prison gates will be sealed for ever. And, to quell the weeping of the abolitionists, these containers need no longer even be referred to as "prisons." Some less offensive euphemism could be found in order to remove them from the latter's attention: a triumph for democracy and reform.

The struggle against prison is therefore a struggle that concerns all of us, not as something separate and specialized, but an essential component of every struggle against Capital and the State. The discourse becomes comprehensible if we enter it as active participants, becoming for a moment one of these comrades in that hall in Bologna so many years ago, with pounding hearts ready to take on the world. Where are they now? We don't know, but we are here, and that is what counts. Let's destroy *all* prisons now!

Jean Weir
London, October 2008

PRISON IS THE MAINSTAY OF THE PRESENT SOCIETY. OFTEN IT does not seem so, but it is.

Our permissive, educative society allows itself to be guided by enlightened politicians and is against any recourse to strong measures. It looks on scandalized at the massacres dotted all over the world map, and seems to be composed of so many respectable citizens whose only concerns are respecting nature and paying as little tax as possible. This society, which considers itself to be far beyond barbarity and horror, has prison on its very doorstep.

Now, the mere existence of a place where men and women are held locked up in opportunely equipped iron cages, watched over by other men and women wielding bunches of keys, a place where human beings spend years and years of their lives doing nothing, absolutely nothing, is a sign of the utmost disgrace, not just for this society but for a whole historical era.

I am writing this introduction in Rebibbia prison and I don't feel like changing a word of the talk that I gave in Bologna a few years ago. If I compare the thickheadedness of the prison institution today with that of my experiences recounted in the text published below, I see that nothing has changed.

Nothing could change. Prison is a sore that society tries to conceal in vain. Like the doctors in the seventeenth century who treated the plague by putting ointment on the sores but left rats running around among the rubbish, today, at every level of the prison hierarchy technicians are trying to cover up this or that horrible aspect of prison, not realizing that the only way to face the latter is to destroy it. We must destroy all prisons and leave not one stone standing, not keep a few around in order to remember them in the way that humanity has done with other constructions that testify to the most atrocious infamy.

Now someone who tends to beat about the bush will ask: how can we destroy prison? How can we get rid of it completely in a society like this, where a bunch of bosses called the State decide for everybody and impose these decisions by force?

So, the best of these squawkers, the quick-witted with hearts of gold, try to mitigate prisoners' suffering by giving them cinema once a week, colored TV, almost edible food, weekly visits, some hope of being released before the end of their sentence and everything else. Of course, these good people want something in exchange. After all, that's not asking too much. They want prisoners to behave and show respect to the warders, acquire the capacity to resist years and years of inactivity and sexual abstinence, undergo psychological treatment by specialized personnel and declare, more or less openly, that they have been redeemed and are capable of returning to the society that expelled them for misbehaving.

I have been a frequenter of prisons for more than a quarter of a century, so can compare a few things. Once prisoners literally lived in an infamous disgusting hole visited by rats and various other creatures. They only saw the light of day for a few minutes, did not have TV and could not even make a cup of coffee in their cells. The situation has certainly improved today. Prisoners [in Italy] can actually make meals, even cakes, in the cell. They have more hours' recreation in a day than they used to get in a month, and can have extra visits and make a few phone calls to the family. They can work for a decent wage (half the average wage outside), watch color TV, have a fridge, a shower, and everything else.

Of course prisoners accept these improvements, they're not stupid. And why not. They also accept paying the price, by showing themselves to be good and condescending, arguing with the guards as little as possible and telling stories to the educators and psychologists who hang around the corridors like shadows, waiting for it to be time to go home and for the end of the month to pick up their salary. Apart from the obvious consequence of lowering the level of conflict in prisons, nobody in this scenario really believes that the prisoner will be re-inserted into so-called civil society. It is a farce that each player recites magnificently.

Let's take the priest for example. If he isn't stupid he knows perfectly well that all the prisoners who go to mass go to meet prisoners from other wings whom they wouldn't otherwise see. He accepts that with the hypocrisy of his trade and gets on with it. Of course, now and again some prisoner will show a sudden faith, enlightenment on the road to Damascus. But this, the priest knows perfectly well, is functional to the treatment for getting out on parole or having a suspended sentence or another of the many benefits provided for by the law but subordinate to the approval of the custodial personnel, educators, psychologists, and also the priest.

What was clear when one was face to face with the police becomes hazy inside. Today nearly all prisoners are losing their identity as such and are accepting permissive changes that are gradually trapping them within a mechanism that promises not so much to redeem them as to let them out a little before the end of their time.

As the attentive reader of this little book will see, there is a line of reasoning that claims to want to "abolish" prison. Now, to abolish means to ablate, i.e. eliminate, an essential component from society. Leaving things as they are, this abolition would be impossible or, if it were to come about, it would turn out to be in the interests of power.

Let's try to explore this. The only way to do something serious about prison is to destroy it. That is no more absurd or utopian than the thesis that wants to abolish it. In both cases the State, for which prison is essential, would have recourse to extreme measures. But specific conditions of a revolutionary character could make the destruction of prison possible. They could create social and political upheaval that would make this utopia come true, due to the sudden absence of the power required for prison to continue to exist.

In the case of abolition, if it were to happen progressively it would mean that the State was providing for prison in a different way. In fact, something of the sort is actually happening. As I will show, prisons are opening up. Political forces that were once quite cut off from them now enter them regularly. There are all kinds of cultural manifestations, cinema, theatre, painting, poetry; all these sectors are hard at work. This opening also requires the prisoners' participation. At first, participation seems to eliminate disparity, allowing everyone to be equal; it means that people don't have to stay locked up in cells all day and gives them the possibility to talk and make their demands heard. And this is true, in that the "new" prison has taken the place of the "old." But not all prisoners are prepared to participate. Some still have their dignity as "outlaws," which they don't want to lose, so they refuse.

I am not proposing the old distinction here between "political" and "common law" prisoners which has never really convinced me. Personally I have always refused—and continue to do so now in the prison where I am writing this introduction—the label of "political" prisoner. I am referring to the "outlaws," those whose lives have been entirely dedicated to living against and beyond the conditions established by law. It is clear that if on the one hand prison is opening up to prisoners who are prepared to participate, it is closing down on those who are not and want to remain "outlaws," even in prison.

Given the advances in control in society, the great potential of information technology in this field and the centralization of the security services and the police, at least at the European level, we can well imagine that those going against the law in the not too distant future really will have the absolute determination of the outlaw.

We can sum up by saying that the project of power for the future is to abolish the traditional prison and open it up to participation, and at the same time create a new, absolutely closed version: a prison with white coats where the real outlaws will end their days. This is the prison of the future, and those who are talking about abolition will be happy, in that in the future these prisons with white coats might not even be called by such a hateful name, but rather clinics for mental patients. Isn't someone who insists on rebelling and affirming their identity as an "outlaw" in defiance of all propositions to participate in society, absolutely mad? And do mad people perhaps not constitute a medical rather than a penitentiary problem?

Such a society, having a greater capacity for social and political control, would call for everyone to collaborate in this repressive project, so would have less need to have recourse to sentencing. The very concept of sentencing would be put in question. Basically, most of the prison population today are people who have committed "crimes" such as taking drugs, drug dealing, petty theft, administrative offenses, etc., which from one moment to the next might no longer be considered such. By removing these people from prison and reducing the probability of more serious offenses such as robbery and kidnapping through increased levels of social control, few actual real crimes will remain. Crimes of passion could very well be dealt with through recourse to house arrest, and that is the intention. And so, who would remain in prison under such conditions? The few thousand individuals who refuse to accept this project, who hate such a choice and refuse to obey or put themselves down. In a word, conscious rebels who continue to attack, perhaps against all logic, and against whom it will be possible to apply specific conditions of detention and "cure" closer to that of an asylum than an actual prison. That is where the logical premise of prison abolition leads us in the final analysis. The State could very well espouse this thesis at some time in the not too distant future.

Prison is the most direct, brutal expression of power, and like power it must be destroyed, it cannot be abolished progressively. Anyone who thinks they can improve it now in order to destroy it in the future will forever be a captive of it.

The revolutionary project of anarchists is to struggle along with the exploited and push them to rebel against all abuse and repression, so also against prison. What moves them is the desire for a better world, a better life with dignity and ethic, where economy and politics have been destroyed. There can be no place for prison in that world.

That is why anarchists scare power.

That is why they are locked up in prison.

Alfredo M. Bonanno

Rebibbia prison, March 20, 1997

Voici le temps des Assassins.
(This is the time of murderers.)

—Arthur Rimbaud

THE PRISON QUESTION IS SOMETHING THAT ANARCHISTS AND the revolutionary movement in general have been involved in for a long time. We come back to it periodically because for many of us it is something that touches us directly, or touches comrades close to us, whom we love.

To know what prison is like and why it exists and functions, or how it might cease to exist, or function better according to one's point of view, is no doubt a very interesting subject. I have heard many talks, conferences and debates in the past, particularly about ten years ago. At that time reality was seen analytically due to a certain Marxism that was boss of the political scene both culturally and practically, and the main aspect of the debate on prison was the "professionalism" with which it was carried on.

One was usually listening to, or imagined one was listening to, someone who knew something about prison. Well, that's not the case here. In fact, I don't know all that much about prison. I'm not aware of knowing much about prison and I'm certainly not a specialist on the subject, and even less someone who has suffered all that much, ...a bit, yes. So, if that is the way you see things, I mean from a kind of professional point of view, don't expect much from this talk. No professionalism, no specific competence. I should say right away that I feel a kind of repulsion, a sense of profound disgust for people who present themselves on a particular subject and split reality up into sectors declaring, "I know all about this subject, now I'll show you." I don't have that competence.

I have had my misfortunes of course, in the sense that I first went to prison over twenty years ago and, in fact, when I found myself locked up in a cell for the first time I found myself in great difficulty. The first thing I wanted to do was destroy the radio, because it was a very loud transmission and after a few minutes locked up in there I felt as though I was going mad. I took off a shoe and tried to smash the object that was making such an obscene din. The noise was coming from an armored box screwed into the ceiling next to a light bulb that was constantly lit. After a few minutes, a head appeared at the peephole of the armored door and said, "Excuse me, what are you doing?" I answered, "I'm trying to..." "—No, that's not necessary, all you have to do is call me, I'm the cleaner, so I switch off the radio from outside and everything's okay." At that moment I discovered what prison was, and is. There, that sums up my specific culture on the subject of prison. Prison is something that destroys you, that seems absolutely unbearable—"how on earth will I be able to survive in here with this thing driving me crazy"...snap, a little gesture, and it's over. This is my professionalism on prison. And it is also a little personal story concerning my imprisonment.

There have been many studies about prison of course, but I know little about them. Bear in mind that these studies have not only been carried out by specialists of the sociology of deviance, but even by prisoners themselves, and funded by the Ministry. One such study concerns Bergamo prison. I saw it and found incredible desire and capacity to do so, who even manage to sell this nonsense off as something interesting. To me this theoretical posing is nothing but sociological gymnastics.

The main supporters of prison, without actually realizing or desiring it, are the prisoners themselves. Just like the worker who sees himself in the dimension of the factory, if he is a factory worker, or in any case in the chains that hold him down. As

Malatesta said, being accustomed to the chains we don't realize that we are able to walk, not thanks to them but in spite of them, because there is something that is unclear. Often, when talking to a prisoner who has done twenty, even thirty years' prison, he will tell you about all the woes of prison life etc., of course, but you also realize that he has a love-hate relationship with the institution, because basically it has *become* his life. And that is part of the problem. So you realize that you cannot work out a critique of prison by starting off from the ideas and experiences that come out of it, because the experience is certainly negative and full of repulsion and hatred of the place, but it is always ambivalent, like all experiences of life. I have lived this myself and I can't explain how I felt it growing inside me. Human beings are not automata, they don't see things in black and white. Well, it happens that the instant you get out of prison you have the sensation that you are leaving something dear to you. Why? Because you know that you are leaving a part of your life inside, because you spent some of your life there which, even if it was under terrible conditions, is still a part of you. And even if you lived it badly and suffered horribly, which is not always the case, it is always better than the nothing that your life is reduced to the moment it disappears. So, even pain, any pain, is better than nothing. It is always something positive, perhaps we can't explain it but we know it, prisoners know it. So they are precisely the first to support prison.

Then there is common sense, this massive stumbling block, that cannot see how it would be possible to do without prison. In fact, this common sense pushes proposals for the abolition of prison up a blind alley, showing them to be ridiculous because such proposals want to have their cake and eat it, whereas it would be far easier to simply say, "prison is necessary in the present state of affairs." How can I put the jeweler's right to safeguard his property before my right to take his jewels at gunpoint, I who have no money and nothing to eat? The two things are a contradiction. How can I overcome this contradiction by putting it at the level of a universal contract or a natural right desired by God, the Devil, Reason, or Kropotkinian animism? The only way to look at the problem is the elementary one: if all goes well, I take the money, if it doesn't I do my time. I have spoken to many robbers and one of the first I met said to me, "Listen, you who can read and write, take a piece of paper and do the sums. How much can I earn in three years working in a factory?" (At the time the factory wage was about 15 million [old lire] a month). And, he continued, "If I do a robbery and it goes well I take more than 15 million: 20, maybe 30. If things go wrong I do three years and I'm back where I started. Moreover, if it does go wrong, I'm not working under a boss who drives me crazy for three years, or in Germany, sleeping in Portacabins. I'm in jail and at least I'm respected here. I'm a bank robber and when I go out into the yard I'm seen as a serious person, not a poor sod that lives from his labor." Frankly, with all my science, I was at a loss for words. What he said didn't sound wrong to me, even at the level of basic economics. And what could I say? "But, you know, you can't violate property." He'd have spat in my face! Or, "The scales are unbalanced, you must set them right," but then for him they had tipped the scales once and for all. As [Johann Gottlieb] Fichte, who knew something about philosophy, or at least he thought so, said, "Whoever has been defrauded of what is due to him on the basis of the social contract has the right to go and take it back." And Fichte was certainly not a revolutionary or even progressive.

Common sense prevents us from imagining society without prison. It does well, in my opinion, because common sense cannot always be ignored, and a society under the present conditions of production, with the existing cultural and political relations, cannot do without prison. To imagine the elimination of prison from the present social context is a fine utopia good only for filling up the pages of books by those who work in the universities and write in the pay of the State.

The rest, in my opinion, is an absolute waste of time, at least for those who understand anything at all. It might be that I didn't quite get these texts about abolishing prison. Yet I seem to have noticed that some of the people who support abolition, whom I actually know, are the same as those who once called themselves, I'm not saying Stalinists, but at least supporters of the chatter of historical materialism on prison, i.e. they supported the analyses of prison as a reality that is strictly linked to production. These same people are for the abolition of prison today because the current ideas are no longer Stalinist or authoritarian but are of an anarchist or at least libertarian nature. Apart from these people's extraordinary capacity for political evolution, which never ceases to amaze me, I insist that, in any case, concepts such as abolition are still stupid, even if they call themselves anarchist. And why not? Can anarchists not talk rubbish? There's nothing strange about that. There's no equation that says anarchist equals intelligent; anarchists are not necessarily intelligent in my opinion. I know many stupid anarchists. And I've encountered many intelligent cops. What's wrong with that? I've never seen anything strange in that.

Yes, the concept doesn't seem difficult because abolition—at least as far as I can see, but perhaps I didn't quite get it, and we are here to clarify our ideas—the abolition of part of something, is an ablation. In other words, I take a part and cut it out. Society, of which prison is an indispensable component today, should therefore take prison and get rid of it like you do with a rotten piece of something. You cut it out and throw it in the dustbin. That is the concept of abolition. Abolish prison and put some other kind of social organization in its place. In order not to be a prison in all but name, it must not foresee sanctions or the application of a sentence, law, the principle of coercion, etc. What they possibly don't want to see is the fact that abolition of prison implies the upturning of the situation that is juridically created between the victim and the perpetrator of the crime, the so-called guilty party. Today, a separation between the victim and the guilty one is carried out, and with prison this separation becomes clear. Victim and guilty party must never meet again, in fact they will forever avoid each other. I will certainly never go to Bergamo to look for the jeweler whose shop I robbed. He would call the police as soon as he saw me, there's no doubt about that.

What happens in the case of abolition? The two protagonists of the "illegal" deed are not kept apart, on the contrary they are put in contact through negotiation. For example, they establish what the damages amount to together and instead of going to prison the person responsible for the "illegal" deed pledges to repay the damage, in money or through work. For example, it seems that there are people who are happy to have their houses painted, I don't know, that sort of thing. In my opinion, these absurdities start off from a philosophical principle that is quite different to that envisaged by the law.

The separation of the "guilty party" from the "victim" also depends on the specific situation, except in cases where this was caused by passion or uncontrollable emotions. In most cases, not only does the guilty one try to escape to save the booty or his skin, he also tries to have as little contact with the victim as possible. Then there is the other aspect of alienation, that which is institutionalized by the intervention of the judge, the lawyer, the court, the prison. So, not only separation from the victim but also from society, with the aftermath of the particular attention paid to re-entry into society. In order to avoid too brusque a contact there are often precise police practices: you leave prison, the police patrol picks you up immediately and takes you off to the police station, and you are identified again. You are free because you have finished your sentence, but they are not satisfied. Hence the expulsion orders from certain towns, etc.

Abolition does not foresee any of this. It is a more complex concept, and cannot be grasped immediately. But there remains this curious logical anomaly: in theory ablation is possible, in practice it is impossible in a social context where prison is obviously an essential component.

The destruction of prison, on the other hand, clearly linked to the revolutionary concept of destruction of the State, exists within a process of struggle. In order for what we said earlier to be fully understood, our discourse must not be based on models of efficiency, as that would distort it. The struggles we participate in and their consequences can never be seen as getting something in exchange for what we do, of necessarily getting results from what we put on the carpet. On the contrary, we are often unable to see the consequences of the struggles we participate in, there is a very wide relational dispersion and the end results cannot be foreseen. We have no idea what might happen as far as other people active in the struggle are concerned, comrades doing different things, changes in relations, changes in awareness, etc. All of these things come later, when we think everything is over.

We are having this discussion here tonight, and for me this is also struggle...Because it is not enough for me just to talk for the pleasure of hearing my own voice, and I am convinced that some new ideas are entering your heads, just as I am experiencing the joy of being here and feeling your physical presence. We are talking about something close to my heart and I will take this gift you are giving me away with me. Just as I think I can give you something to take away with you that might bear fruit at some time in the future, in another situation, another context. And that has nothing to do with quantity or efficiency. If it means anything at all it means something in practice, in the things we do, in the transformation we bring about, not in the abstract realm of theory or utopia. That is what I am trying to say about the destruction of prison. Because as soon as we put ourselves in this logic and begin to act, even in discussions like this evening, or with other things that we won't discuss here but could go into tomorrow or at some time in the near future, we begin to transform reality. Prison becomes one element of this transformation, and by transformation we mean destruction— partial destruction in view of the final destruction of the State. I am aware that this concept might seem too rash or too philosophical. But as soon as we start to think about it, it becomes clear because it becomes a basis for all the actions we carry out every day and for the way we behave with those close to us, those we relate to and who put up with us every day, as well as those whom we see from time to time.

The revolutionary project is also this. There is no such thing as separate worlds, the world I live with my companion, with my children, with the few revolutionary comrades I have met in my life who want to overturn the world, all absolutely separate. That's not so, it's not like that. If I am a bastard in my sexual relations, I cannot be a revolutionary, because these relations immediately spread themselves into the wider context. I might fool one, two, three people, then the fourth will take me to task and I can't deceive them. There must necessarily be unity of intent, that elective affinity that links me to all my actions, in any context whatsoever, in everything I do, which I cannot separate.. If I am a bastard, it will come out sooner or later.

But let's get back to our argument which we seem to have left a long way off.

Let's look at the whole question of prison, the sentence, the judiciary that supports and makes the sentence possible, and I think that most of you here know more about this than me.

I think it would be good if we were to agree on a very simple line of thought: the concept of the sentence is based on one essential principle—the privation that a given person suffers for not having behaved according to pre-established rules. Now, if we look carefully here, we see that this concept applies to many things, even interpersonal relations. But it only concerns particular sanctions when one finds oneself faced with the law, a State structure that is capable of enforcing the sanction according to pre-established rules, or at least within the ambit of these rules.

What does the State want from the sentence? Not just the State today, which we know to some extent, but the State in general as it has developed over at least the past three hundred years. What does Power, which has not always defined itself as the State, want to attain? In the first place it wants to make the so-called guilty party submit to a higher level of physical control than is usual in the so-called free society.

I repeat, I don't have any specific competency in this field but from what I have read, and it isn't much and perhaps not even up to date, the process of control is now mainly entrusted to information technology, data gathering, etc. Basically, the universal recording of our details that is being carried out by the authorities (for example I have seen that they are even monitoring us through our electricity bills) is, so to speak, a roundup strategy that will end up netting all the fish, so only a few will manage to escape. But this monitoring is only an approximation. Some countries are far ahead in this field, with very efficient procedures, yet even in these countries there is still some space for extra-legal, even if not exactly "outlaw," activity in concrete terms.

The project of power is certainly omnipresent and intends to include everyone in this data gathering. The more effective preventive control is, the more the State becomes boss of the territory. It is no coincidence, for example, that there is so much talk about the Mafia, to the point of overstepping the boundaries between myth and reality, where it is not clear where one begins and the other ends. I don't know if it's worth going into this question which, although fascinating, is not very important in my opinion. However, there can be little doubt that this is being exploited at the moment, also for the mysterious aim of reaching an equilibrium between the political parties... But, apart from all this, the establishment of strong preventive control should make prison, at least as we know it, far less necessary. So, the function of the sentence is control, and the more this function spreads to the point of becoming preventive, the more prison will tend to change.

We must bear in mind that prison is quite different today to what it was twenty years ago. It has changed more over the past ten years than it did over the last hundred, and the whole process is still moving at this rate. Today, the so-called model prisons are not all that different from the maximum security prisons of the 1980s. I don't want to split hairs here, but, in fact, although there were particular forms of control in the maximum security prisons, that was not the main difference. I was held in a maximum security wing similar to Fossombrone at a time when such places existed, and was under article 90 for a few months, so I know what it means: strip searches every day, dozens of guards outside the cell door every morning, and everything else. These aspects are certainly terrible but they are not the main thing. There are no effectively maximum security prisons left [in Italy] today. Nowadays they may have fewer hours' sociality in some places, the exercise period may only be allowed in two's or three's, but in the future everything could get much worse. Why?

When control covers the whole social territory the so-called spontaneous prison population will be greatly reduced. Many "crimes" will be declassified and there will be less institutional imprisonment (possibly through the use of electronic devices such as "Trasponder," electronic bracelets that set off an alarm if you go beyond the assigned perimeter, and so on).[1] Then, yes, there will be a real change in the prisons that remain. Here isolation, psychological torture and white coats will take the place of bloodstains on the wall, and science will be applied to obtain the total destruction of the "outlaws" who have no intention of negotiating with the State. That is how we see prison evolving, and I believe that studies are already being carried out on the subject. There would no longer be any need to keep on calling the places of physical annihilation that remain "prisons," in fact they could be called anything at all. For example, it would be sufficient to qualify someone's behavior as insane in order to have them locked up in a mental asylum. And if the law prevents us from calling these places asylums and they are called "Jesus Christ," they will still be places where people are being killed slowly.

So, as I said before, the law wants to control but it also wants to bring the offender, i.e. he who has marked himself with breaking the rules, back to "normality." It wants to apply an orthopedic technique to those who have behaved *differently*, draw them into the system and render them innocuous. It wants to ensure that this deformed behavior will not repeat itself, and prevent any damage, or presumed damage, to the community.

There is a great contradiction here. Although it no longer fully subscribes to the orthopedic ideology—and we will see within what limits it does accept it—the judiciary realize that the sentencing actually makes the "different" more dangerous. So, on the one hand they want to rehabilitate deviants through the use of the sentence and on the other this makes them more dangerous. In other words, it gives the individual access to a process that makes him become more of a danger to society, which might have been quite accidental up until then.

1   For more on this topic see *Prison By Any Other Name: The Harmful Consequences of Popular Reforms* by Maya Schenwar and Victoria Law. — *Detritus*

The distinction I mentioned is based on the existence of a not clearly identifiable minority of rebels that constitute the real community of outlaws inside the prisons. These irreducible individuals have none of the political characteristics that a debate in the 1960s tried to pin on them.

I think that any distinction now between "political" and "common" law prisoners that existed for a long time and caused so much damage in my opinion, no longer has any reason to exist. This distinction was sometimes even proposed and supported by anarchists in the 1970s and the first half of the 1980s. At that time it was adopted by power in order to maintain a certain equilibrium. For example, when you called the jailer, the politicals would shout "*agente*" (officer) and the other prisoners "*guardia*" (guard). So as soon as you heard someone shouting "*agente*" you knew that they were a comrade. There, something so simple created a distinction that, moved into other areas often came to be distorted by power and transformed into an instrument of recuperation. This distinction between political and common law prisoners was never really valid anyway in my opinion, except for those who wanted to use a part of the prison population for their own ends: the growth of the militant—military and militant—party, the possibility of building up power relations inside the prison and the plan to use the "lumpenproletarian" prisoners. In a few cases, certain elements were even used to carry out low works of justice, in plain words, as murderers to kill people. Have I made myself clear? This has taken place. We are talking of an historic responsibility that some of the personalities who once led the old Marxist-Leninist combatant parties and are in free circulation today took upon themselves. Some of our own comrades were also killed that way. Not because this distinction was made, but by an instrumentalization of its consequences. It put so-called common prisoners at the disposition of some of those who defined themselves political prisoners in order to increase their bargaining power inside the prison or with the Ministry in order to get certain results. This ran parallel to the militaristic practice of the management of power or "counterpower" outside (each to their own taste) and the central importance of the industrial workers, guided by the party that was to lead them to their emancipation. These are all dinosaurs today as far as I am concerned. They're not in touch with reality as I see it, at least I hope they're not, maybe I'm wrong.

It might be useful to pause here for a moment in order to clarify our opposition to any struggle for amnesty, something that raised more than a few objections a number of years ago, even among anarchists.

The situation has changed now concerning relations between the prisoners who insist on positions wrongly defined as *irreducible* and those who have entered into negotiation with the State. At that time, 1985–86 I think, I published a book, *And We Will Always be Ready to Storm the Gates of Heaven Again*, which many considered to be a criticism of the validity of a "struggle for amnesty." The prevailing idea at the time was contained in [Oreste] Scalzone's so-called manifesto which carried, precisely, the proposal of a struggle for amnesty and this was also made by some of the anarchist movement, with the usual lack of comprehension. But that was, let's say, a secondary effect. It wasn't the main aim of the book. The important thing, still today, is that nobody has the right to say, "Comrades, the war is over." First, nobody declared this war in the first place and so, until proved otherwise, no one can decree the end of it. No State declared the war, nor did any armed group have the idea of declaring one. The reasoning is characteristic of the militarist logic, the logic of opposing groups that decide to call a truce at some point. No one can tell us that "the war is over," even less so when the reason for doing so is simply to justify one's own desistence.

If I don't feel like carrying on, given that no one can be forced to continue if they don't feel like it, I say, "My friends, a man is made of flesh and blood, he can't go on forever. So, if I don't feel I can make it, what must I do? Sign a piece of paper? I don't carry out impure actions, I don't get comrades arrested, I'm simply making a declaration of my own desistence." I have always considered this to be a legitimate position, because nobody can be obliged to carry on if they don't feel up to it. But desistence is no longer legitimate if, in order to justify it, I come out with the statement, "I can't carry on because the war is over." No, I no longer agree, because where does that lead us? To all the others both inside and outside prison for whom it isn't true that the war is over, or for whom this concept is dubious, but end up believing it because everybody is saying so. And, desisting or not desisting, they end up reaching the same conclusion. It would be quite indecorous for me to push others to desist in order for me to justify my own personal decision to give up the struggle.

Now, conditions are radically different today, not in the sense that this indecorousness no longer exists, but in the sense that it is out of date as other attitudes prevail. They no longer say "The war is over," which moreover would be unfounded as they should really say "The war never began; *our* war wasn't really a social war at all." But most of them prefer to dedicate themselves to astrology or, sometimes, to assisting prisoners. Yet, if you like, some of them might say, "Perhaps we were wrong about some things, perhaps other ideas should have been accepted in some of the debates that took place around the beginning of the 1970s." That would be a fine critical approach. I'm thinking of one meeting at Porto Marghera where, among other things, the killing of Calabresi [supercop responsible for the death of anarchist Giuseppe Pinelli in 1969 when he was; "suicided" from the fourth floor window of the Milan central police station] was under discussion. This was a very important debate, which nobody talks about because hardly anybody knows anything about it. Here, for the first time in Italy, two positions appeared concerning this action...But perhaps not everybody is interested in these questions...Well, between astrology and Welfarism, another hypothesis has appeared, "It's necessary to start the war again, but with different weapons, not with the critique of arms, but with the arms of critique." They are ready to take on the world again, with words. As far as I know, this chatter concerns the management of daily life. So, centers for the elaboration of chatter are appearing everywhere: centers for the elaboration of information, radio stations (very important, where between some strange music and a pseudo-cultural discussion, concepts of taking over the territory are pushed through), squats verging on legalization or verging on survival, closed up in themselves in the miserable ghetto. In this way dreams of controlling the territory are reawakened. Through revarnished old concepts, the same old centralized, more or less militant party (but you can't say that any more) management is getting into gear, and a new pattern is emerging. This is all chatter for the time being: if they are roses they will blossom. I think that's what is happening, we don't need to give precise indications, we all know what I'm talking about. This chatter has some interesting aspects: the recycling of old caryatids in disuse...Of course, me too I'm an old caryatid, for goodness sake...But I still have some ideas that seem to me to be interesting...that's just my opinion, I might be wrong.

There is still a nucleus of comrades in prison who are not prepared to bargain with the State. Our solidarity can go to these comrades, but that's not enough. It can't be enough for someone with centuries of prison on their backs. Detailed proposals are necessary, indications setting out the concrete destruction of prisons. At the present time, at least so it seems to me, there is no sign of any project based on the destruction of prisons. It is necessary to start all over again. If you insist on a kind of cohabitation with power, you increase desistence from the struggle. And it is not just a question of a model of intervention that I disagree with but which I might take into consideration while doing other things, if I could. Unfortunately, this whole mechanism is starting up again and could give certain results, results that are not acceptable to us, but which in themselves are quite legitimate. That is why the situation is different today. On the other hand, you won't get far with demonstrations of solidarity, such as, for example, 100,000 postcards addressed to the President of the Republic. These things are usually a waste of time, they have never meant much. Yes, letters, telegrams, might help comrades to feel they haven't been abandoned, because it's nice for someone in prison to get letters of solidarity, etc. Then, within certain limits, that can make an impression on the prison authorities and on the individual screw, who when he passes to control you at night might not keep the light on for three seconds, but only one, because he's scared and says to himself, "This one got twenty telegrams today, maybe one of his friends will be waiting for me outside and split my head open," very important things, for goodness' sake, I'm not denying it. It's a question of doing something, applying pressure, even minimal, in order to create a more important deterrent perhaps, but looking at things realistically I'm afraid these comrades still have many years ahead of them.

The debate about amnesty was not a simple theoretical exercise, however. It soon became an instrument for realizing certain practical actions and suggesting a way of intervening on the question of prison. It was, and continues to be, important in trying to pose the problem of prison from a revolutionary point of view. The acceptance of the struggle for amnesty was a macroscopic mistake, in my opinion. It was also proposed inconsiderately and ignorantly by more than a few anarchists who, not knowing what to do, and not being aware of the risks implicit in such a choice, decided to support it. It was a serious political and revolutionary mistake which, I have to say in all honesty, I didn't make.

For example, the position regarding the Gozzini law[2] changed in relation to the justification of the struggle for amnesty. Such choices had consequences for the supporters of revolutionary authority. Clearly if somebody says that prison changes deterministically according to the changes in society, any attempt by the enemy to adjust my behavior to the historical evolution of reality, for example the Gozzini law, is all right by me. So I accept it, in view of the struggle moving into other sectors. The same goes for trade union bargaining. So I don't see why it should be any different for prison. What seems like innocent sociological theory becomes a precise political choice involving the lives and future of thousands of comrades in prison. We have always maintained that we are against amnesty, or rather a *struggle for amnesty* (which are two different things, when they give us an amnesty of their own accord we'll certainly take it).

Now let's come back to the contradictions inherent in the

2   This was a 1986 prison reform law that instituted early release for good behavior, work-release programs, holidays at home, etc. — Detritus

concept of the sentence and the various ways in which it is applied. The theoretical debate on prison still contains the basic contradictions seen above, which are really unsolvable.

In fact, these contradictions have become more acute in recent times. Not that they didn't exist before. But the function of the sentence, the structure meting it out and prison itself—let's say around or up until 1500—was to hold people until given sanctions were applied. Or they functioned purely as separation, to keep certain people away from their social context. Piombi, in the seventeenth century, as you can read in Casanova's *Memoires,* was a prison in Venice that was self-managed by the inmates. There were no custodians inside the prison walls, only outside, and that was one of the worst prisons of the era. But already with the Piombi we are later than 1500, we are fully into the seventeenth century.

So the old prison had a different function. The aim of the modern prison is to "recuperate"—we are talking about the theory behind it—to bring the individual back to a condition of normality. So prison has had two functions, the old one where it was simply a place in which the individual was stored while awaiting his or her fate (the death penalty, mutilation, exclusion from the social context, a journey to the Holy Land, which was equivalent to the death penalty given the difficulties of such a journey in 1200–1300) and the modern one. Between these there was the introduction of the so-called workhouses at the beginning of the 1700s, with the aim of getting prisoners to work.

At a purely cultural level there was a theoretical debate that we don't need to go into here. Suffice it to say that prison structures such as Bentham's Panopticon, where a single custodian could control all the wings at once—and bear in mind that similar structures still exist in many prisons today—saw the light at the same time as the industrial revolution. Some see a historical parallel between these two developments, the figure of the modern prisoner emerging alongside that of the worker in the early industrial plants. The industrial condition develops and transforms, and has been the object of much criticism, whereas the concept of naturalism in law remains, and giusnaturalism [a Natural Law-ism, if you will] is still at the root of the sacrality of the norm.

It doesn't really make any difference whether the sacrality of the norm originates from the positivist doctrine, from God, from a law intrinsic to the development of animated beings, or is intrinsic to the development of the History of man and the vicissitudes of human reason (historical finalism). Anybody supporting any one of these theses is always looking for a foundation upon which to erect their own behavioral construction, their own castle of rules. Once the latter is built, anyone who finds themselves outside the fortified circle becomes a legitimate candidate for prison, segregation, exclusion, or death, as the case may be.

Now, the thesis that interests us most, because it is still an object of debate and study today, is that concerning natural law, i.e. a law that is natural to reason as it develops throughout history. This concept is important because it allows for some interesting modifications, that is to say it has not been crystallized once and for all in the will of God, but changes according to events in history. It developed fully with the Enlightenment in the eighteenth century, has all the limitations of the philosophical interpretation of the time, and contains two essential elements: first history, then reason. History is seen to be progressive, moving from a state of chaos, animality, or danger towards one that is safer and more humane. [Giovanni] Bovio said, "History is moving towards anarchy," and many anarchists, at least of my generation, have repeated that. I have never believed it possible to draw such a straight line on this question. I am not at all convinced that history is moving towards anarchy. There is another shadow in this beautiful enlightened, then positivist, then idealist, then historicist discourse, that runs parallel to it. All of these theories were elaborated in the academia of power, in universities where philosophy and history are studied, places where the suppliers of the State prisons are hard at work. And what is this other shadow? It is the Shadow of Reason. Why is Reason always right? I don't know. It is always right to sentence someone. People are sentenced to the electric chair with reason, nobody is sentenced to death without reason, there are a thousand reasons for sentencing people to death. A sentence without reason doesn't exist. I have been in prison many times, with reason, their reason.

It has been said that Nazism, realized in Germany in the 1930s–40s, was an explosion of irrationality, that is, of a lack of reason. Well, I have never believed such a thing. Nazism was the extreme consequence of the application of reason, i.e. the Hegelian reason of the objective spirit that realizes itself in History, taken to its natural conclusion. The most logical discourse in this sense was made by an Italian philosopher, Gentile, at a conference in Palermo where he made reference to the moral force of the truncheon. By striking in the name of reason, the truncheon is always right, and State violence is always ethical because the State is ethical.

All this might sound stupid, but it isn't because it constitutes the foundation of so-called modern progressivism. We have seen this in the Communist Party, the workers' party, in Marxist so-called revolutionary movements, and also on the Right, in right-wing movements. Whereas the Right, for its own reasons of identity, wrapped itself up in conventional irrationalism (flags, symbols, discourses on destiny, blood, race, etc.), the former packaged themselves in another variety: progress, history, the future, the proletariat that was to defeat the bourgeoisie, the State that was to extinguish itself. And, I might add, more than a few anarchists tagged on to this discourse, going along with this enormous metaphysical and ideological swindle. They simply pointed out that history was not moving towards the extinction of the State but towards anarchy and that it was necessary to extinguish the State right away in order to reach anarchy more quickly. This ideological subtlety did not move the content of this journey an inch from the Marxist one. And it never entered anyone's head that it was the discourse of reason, and that it might be a swindle and serve as a basis and an alibi for building a wall around the *different*.

That is why it is necessary to look at the optimism of the anarchists—for example Kropotkin's—more deeply and critically, in order to see the limitations of this way of thinking. It is important to see the equivocation of Kropotkin's "seed beneath the snow," as well as those of other comrades of the anarchist positivist tendency. Everything that I'm saying here might seem far from the question of prison—on the contrary, this is exactly the theoretical and philosophical territory in which prison finds its justification.

We should also look at Malatesta's voluntarism, which seems to be the opposite but fails to come up with any solutions unless it is inserted within the "objective" deterministic development of history in the direction of anarchy. I might have limitations, my personal capacity might be circumscribed, but history is moving towards anarchy anyway, so if it doesn't come about now it will some time in the future. We should also take a look at the limitations of Stirner's individualism, something we tried to do at the recent meeting in Florence. We need to see if such limitations really exist and if so, what they are, obviously being very different from those of Malatesta and Kropotkin.

So, what conclusions can we draw at this point? Prison is not an abuse of power, it is not an exception, it is normal. The State builds prisons so that it can put us in them. In so doing it is not doing anything strange, it is simply doing its job. The State is not a prison State, it is the State, that's all. In the same way that it expresses itself through economic and cultural activity, political management and the management of free time, it deals with the management of prison. These elements are not separate, it is impossible to talk about prison on its own, it wouldn't make sense because it would be taking one element out of context. On the other hand, if this element is put into its proper context, and that is exactly what the specialist cannot do, the discourse changes. That is why we started off with the problem of specialization, because the specialist is only able to talk about his own subject. "Given that I know something about prison, I don't see why I should talk about anything else."

I believe that collective experiences, if this concept still means anything, are composed of so many individual moments.

Woe betide if we were to obliterate these individual moments in the name of a superior one, that which the Marxists defined as subsumption. Subsumption of society, never! These terroristic processes must be absolutely condemned. The individual has a moment that is his or hers and the prisoner has his or her moment, which is not the same as that of another prisoner. I absolutely disagree with those who say that I, who have been in prison, struggle more effectively than someone who has not. No, because I struggle differently from someone who has never been in prison and just as differently from one who has done more time than me, and so on. And, viceversa, I could meet a comrade who is capable of making suggestions to me, of making me understand, feel, imagine, or dream a different kind of struggle, even if he has never been in prison. No specialization. Remember the first things that were said this evening: no professionality, no talk of professors, even less professors of prison matters. Fortunately, there is no specialization here, we are not at university.

We are all individuals who seek each other, who meet, disperse, come together again, moving on the basis of affinity, also transitory, which can disappear or intensify. We are like a multitude of atoms in movement, which have a very strong capacity for reciprocal penetration. It is not a question, as [Gottfried Wilhelm] Leibniz said, of monads without windows. We are not isolated, we have our individual value, all individuals do. Only by keeping this ineliminable moment constantly present is it possible to talk of society, or the capacity to act, move and live together, otherwise any society at all would be a prison. If I must sacrifice even a tiny part of my individuality in the name of the *Aufhebung*—"overcoming" in the Hegelian sense of the term—in the name of an abstract principle...even anarchy, even freedom, then I don't agree. Prison is certainly an extreme condition and so, like all total conditions, total institutions, it shows one's true fabric clearly. It is like pulling a piece of cloth as far as it can go, and just before it tears apart the weave begins to appear. There, the individual who submits to the most violent conditions reveals the cloth of which he or she is made. Maybe he or she will discover things about themselves that they would never have imagined in other situations. But this starting point is important and fundamental: no element, idea, dream or utopia can take away this individual moment, nor can the latter be sacrificed to any of the former.

But let's come back to our argument. Prison is the normality of the State, and we, who live under the State with our daily lives regulated by its pace and times, are living in a prison. In my opinion this has been incorrectly but interestingly defined as an immaterial prison. That is to say, it is not visible as such. It does not enclose us in such a direct, shocking way as the walls of a prison do. It is nevertheless a real prison, in that we are forced to submit to and adopt models of behavior that we didn't decide upon ourselves, but have been imposed from outside, about which we can do very little.

But prison is also a construction. It is a place, an ideology, a culture, a social phenomenon. That is, it has a specific identity, so if on the one hand we bring it out of this specificity, we cannot at the same time dilute it into society, and simply say, "We are all in prison, my situation was no different when I passed through that wretched door and found myself in an empty cell with a loud radio blaring." I felt a trauma at the moment I walked through that cell door and heard someone lock it behind me. This trauma exists, it's not purely psychological, it also consists of a fellow with a bunch of keys that jangle continuously, the noise of which you carry with you for the rest of your life. You never forget it, it's something that rings in your ears, even at night when you're asleep, that noise of the keys, someone locking the door on you. This fact of closing the door is, I believe, one of the most horrifying things that one human being can do to another. For me someone who holds a key in his hand and locks a human being behind a door, no matter what the latter might have done, for me anyone who closes that door is an absolutely contemptible person, one about whom it is impossible to talk about in terms of human fraternity, human features and so on. Yet there are moments when you need this individual, when a psychological mechanism connected to solitude lets loose. When you are alone, in your hole...You've been alone for a month, a month and a half, two months. The days pass and you don't see anyone, sometimes you hear incredible noises, at other times nothing, and you hear a footstep there outside. You know it is his footstep. You are absolutely convinced that this is the worst, most contemptible person on earth. Yet at a certain point you stand behind the door and wait for him like a lover because when that despicable person passes he throws you a glance that reminds you that you are a human being. Because he too has two legs, two arms, and two eyes. At a certain point you see him differently. You no longer see the uniform, and you say to yourself, "Humanity still exists after all."

That is what that hole, that little cell, leads to, so you now have something specific that can no longer be seen as the dilution of prison into daily life. That is why prison is not immaterial. That is why prison is both a specific, architectonic structure, and is at the same time diffused. We are all in prison, but prison is also something different. But we must not only see it as something different because if we did we would cease to understand it.

I understand that all this might seem contradictory at first. But that is just an impression. If you think about it, it is no more contradictory than anything else.

The sentence, we said, is the mechanism that the so-called important philosophers...think of what Kant said about the sentence...this great philosopher said something horrendous... He said, "On an island there is a community, and this community dissolves itself and everybody goes away, only one man remains, a murderer, the last to kill a man. Now the community has broken up, there is absolutely nothing to safeguard, there is no longer a common good, there is nothing left to revive, well, that man must still do his sentence." This is what Kant said, the philosopher who opened up the perspective of modern historicism. Bah!

Anyway...So, the sentence, what does it do? According to theoreticians of every hue, it restores the equilibrium that has been upset, it redresses a balance. But what does the sentence really do? It does something else. First of all it precipitates the individual into a condition of uncertainty. That is, anyone facing such a construction, such an efficient mechanism, faces something bigger than himself. This mechanism is composed of lawyers, judges, carabinieri, police, house searches, pushing and pulling, curses, being stripped naked, flexions—once there used to be anal inspections, which anyone who hasn't been subjected to can't imagine—the conditions of detention in the prison...That is the sentence. You are still at the beginning, you still haven't been accused of anything yet, just a few words on a piece of paper bearing an article of the penal code that you don't even understand, but already the sentence enters your blood and becomes part of you. And how does it become part of you? By putting you in a condition of uncertainty. You don't know what's going to happen to you. You can be the most hardened criminal and find yourself in that state of uncertainty, and I know that because I have spoken to people who are apparently in control, people who, when they come into prison, greet the officer in charge, greet this one and that one, but when they go to bed and put their head on the pillow, start to cry. Because the situation is like that, when you come to find yourself in these conditions it's not easy to see how it's all going to end. I've also spoken to many comrades, we have joked together about the situation in prison, but we couldn't deny that we had been placed in a situation of uncertainty where you don't know what to expect the next day...And this condition of uncertainty is perhaps the essential element, the one at the root of all the syndromes, all the specific illnesses, everything that emerges from time in prison. You will be in a condition of uncertainty all the time you are inside. In fact, up until three minutes before you go through the last gate—bear in mind that there are about twenty between your cell door and the outside one—you don't know whether, exactly two meters away from the last gate, a revolt will break out inside, you'll get involved in it and you're lost; you can start talking again twenty years on. So, this uncertainty is practically inside you, you know it's inside you, and you can't say, "Okay, after all I'm a revolutionary, all this doesn't affect me: prison, death, twenty years, two months..." comrades, that's bullshit. It's bullshit that I've said, me too, to give myself courage, and also to give courage to others, the family, my mother, my father, who were old and were brokenhearted by the visits. When I went to prison the first time they cried, poor things. These are difficult situations, and you project uncertainty towards the outside, you project it on to those who love you, your children, on a whole situation that doesn't disappear with chatter. I remember when, precisely finding myself in isolation for the first time, twenty-five years ago, I started to sing anarchist songs...and I hate anarchist songs. How did I manage to sing these songs in there? I was singing to give myself courage, like a child that starts to whistle or tell fairy stories so as not to be scared in the dark.

The other element, which I experienced palpably, was the deformation of communication. You can't make it to communicate. In order to be able to say something, let's say to change your lawyer, a whole bureaucratic procedure must be gone through: in the evening you have to stick a piece of paper on the armored door of your cell saying that you want to go to the registry office next day. The next day they call you, and you set off to the office. Calculating, let's say, that it's about seventy-five meters away, you think you'll only be a few minutes, but no! It can take from ten minutes to an hour and a half to cross these seventy-five meters, and, like an idiot, you wait behind each door for some angel in uniform to come and open it for you, trac-trac, and you pass the first, second, third, fourth obstacle and everything else. This changes your world completely. What does it change? It changes your whole conception of time and space. It sounds easy, because we cope with this concept like we do with money, like coins that we use every day. But it's not so simple, because time is not what is marked by the clock: that is absolute time, Newton's time, that has been determined once and for all. Alongside this time there is that of a French philosopher, and this is known as the real duration, that's to say, there is time in the sense indicated by Saint Augustine, time as consciousness, as the duration of our consciousness. That is waiting. We measure waiting by the beat of our sensations, and its duration is not at all equal to the absolute time of the clock.

Once clocks were forbidden in prison, now, since the prison reform in 1974, they are allowed. And it's worse, in my opinion.

Once you never knew what time it was, you guessed it with the sun, or with the prison routine, which constituted a "natural" clock, an institutional clock, hence you knew that at half past seven the armored door would be opened and the day would begin. The noise they make in opening that door has its historically recognizable function, which has developed in various ways throughout time. While doing some research on the Inquisition, I found instructions in a manual of 1600 on how to open the door in cases where the Confratelli della Compagnia dei Bianchi, the ones with the white hoods that is, had to take a condemned prisoner to the scaffold. The Spanish Inquisition also existed in Sicily, so they were well organized. Those belonging to this Compagnia dei Bianchi had the job of assisting condemned prisoners during the three days preceding execution. One of their tasks was to ensure that they were ready to be brought to justice, and how did they do that? By inventing a particular technique: they acted as though they were about to take the prisoner to the scaffold. They woke him up early, made a lot of noise, marched in groups with all those entrusted with this operation, the halberdiers, etc...But it wasn't true, it was merely an atrocious staging, simply to see how the poor devil would react. If they reacted properly, i.e. didn't go crazy, they were considered ready for the final operation. So, opening an armored door isn't like opening just any door. These well-built young men, instructed in Parma, had received particular dispositions: the armored door is to be opened with extremely violent blows, the sleeping prisoner must jump up in the air. From that moment he must think, "There, the world of dreams is over, now the institution begins, now they are telling me what to do..." Half past seven, you don't go out, you go out at half past eight, in other words, you do everything according to the prison routine, which is obviously what they want.

For example, I don't know, something important...the passage of time is also marked by other things: the milk arrives in the morning (I have thought a lot about these little things, anyway there's nothing else to do in prison so what do you do? You think,) then they bring you an egg or two at ten, then at half past ten or eleven the fruit, then at twelve o'clock lunch, then at two they bring you something else, I don't know, some jam, why? Because that way the time passes, they regulate it for you. The arrival of the food is an event, you frame it within this segregative context and that is what your life boils down to.

All this seems nonsense, but in my opinion it is science, real prison science. What do the so-called prison operators who think they know everything, know about all this? First of all, the university professor has never been in prison. Normally those who take an interest in prison don't have the faintest idea of what it really is. Let's leave aside law professors, who don't even know what they are talking about, poor things. We are talking about prison workers who, the closer they seem to get to the inside of prison the less they possibly understand about it. Lawyers and judges yes, they have been inside prisons, but where? In the external part, in the visitor's rooms. Apart from exceptional cases where a superintendent from the court comes into the wing (but he only comes into the wing, not the cells), lawyers and judges don't normally know what a prison is. I'll go further, even the prison workers, the psychologists, social workers, every species of cop, don't know what prison is. In fact, what is their job? They go into rooms that are reserved for them, call the prisoner, have a fine discussion, then go home and eat their dinner. And, moreover, even the screws don't know what prison is, and can I tell you that from personal experience. For example, when I was in Bergamo prison and the other prisoners and I, within the limits of our abilities, organized—we didn't call it a revolt, but a kind of protest—because they were taking out the plugs we used to block the holes that the screws had made in the toilets to control us even there. All prisoners block these holes as best they can, with anything they can lay their hands on: paper, pieces of wood, hanging towels and a hundred other things. Usually these defences are left alone, but sometimes the governor in Bergamo gave the order to get rid of them, so the screws pushed them out with a pencil. In answer to our protest the governor replied, "Why are you making such a fuss about nothing, after all we are all men." What, we are all men? "You are the governor and I am the prisoner and I don't want the guard looking at me when I'm in the toilet." So the governor thought that the problem was something trivial. But this barracks camaraderie showed that, although he was the governor of a prison, he had no idea what prison is. Because I do not go to the toilet along with my cell mate, a prisoner like myself, a companion of mine whom you certainly can't, in terms of humanity, friendship and personal relationship, compare to a prison governor, that's obvious. And when the toilet was in the cell, one invented a thousand expedients to find the way to use it alone. The toilet used to be right inside the cell. When I was in prison for the first time, in Catania nearly a quarter of a century ago, I got work registering the prisoners' accounts, and I noticed that many prisoners consumed a huge amount of S. Pellegrino magnesium. When I asked why, they explained that by taking this purgative every week their shit didn't smell, or at least it did less. What does that show us? That the governor and the screws have no idea about what prison is. Because to understand prison, you must be on the *other* side of the door when the guard locks it. There is the question of the key, without the key it's all theory.

So, to get back to the point. Of course, prison is composed of the walls, the cop with the machine gun patrolling them, the exercise yard, the mist that descends on the yard and you don't know where you are, what planet you're on, whether you're in exile, on the moon, etc. But, basically, prison is the cell. And you can be alone in that cell or with others, and these are two separate conditions and two different kinds of suffering. Because yes, we are strong, etc., but I have done prison in isolation, and it's no joke. The last time I did almost two years alone, and it was hard. Perhaps for others it is even harder, or at least it is hard in a different way because the animal man behaves strangely in seclusion and so...This is a rough outline of the problems with prison, told lightly, and I won't go into certain other questions.

I had made a note of some other problems but they are not very important. I just want to mention a couple of things, first the smell. Prison has a particular smell that you never forget. You smell it in the morning. I remember, it's a smell that you find in three other places: bars when they open in the morning, billiard rooms, and brothels. In places where the human animal finds itself in particular conditions of suffering there is a particular odor, and prison has this smell and you never forget it, you notice it most in the morning when they open the armored doors, don't ask me why. The other problem is noise, the noise is really something terrible, there's no way you can get used to it. It's not just the music, the Neapolitan songs that torture you. You can't describe it, it's something horrendous. Whereas a problem of secondary importance, at least as far as I could see, and not only from my own personal experience, was the problem of sexual desire; this is not such a problem as it might seem from outside. I saw the prisoners' response to a questionnaire sent round by the ministry about fifteen years ago concerning the eventuality of setting up a system of so-called love hours, let's say, with one's legitimate partner, and it was almost completely negative.

Now let's look at the final part of the question, if you are not too dazed. What can the perspective of prison be? That is, in what way is power trying to restructure prison conditions which, obviously, are never static? Prison is uncertain by definition, so you never know what's going to happen. This uncertainty is also ambivalent as far as the rules are concerned. There is a law that says that the prisoner must be given a copy of the prison rules when he or she arrives, in order to read and respect them, if they want. In some prisons, like the Dozza in Bologna, for example, they give a three page extract, but the actual rules are a beast of 150 pages. So incredible things happen. If someone gets hold of all the rules and reads them carefully they can end up creating problems for the institution.

I said prison is something that is constantly undergoing profound transformation and, in my opinion (this is my personal idea), is moving towards an opening, that is, it is tending to open up and have people participate. In the 1970s it took you about an hour to make a fried egg or a coffee in your cell, because you had to make a kind of construction with empty match boxes covered in silver paper from cigarette packets, then put solid gas under it, then light this thing, always messing about with this alchemy near the toilet because there were no tables or chairs. You had to fold up the bed in the morning

so there was a kind of platform to sit on. There is a considerable difference between these primordial conditions and those
of today where there are even structures where you can cook in
the judicial prisons as well as the penal institutions (the latter
are even better equipped and more "open").

The reform has been approved. This reform has certainly
improved prison conditions to some extent, of course. It has
created a few extra moments of sociality, made other things
worse, and led to greater disparity between prisoners. The
Dozza, for example, is a model prison. Built as a special high
security prison, it is now being used as a normal one and it is
infinitely worse than the old San Giovanni. I have been in both
and can honestly say that the Dozza is worse. But whereas there
were bars over the windows at San Giovanni, then the metal
grid behind the bars, then the ventilation grid, in the Dozza
there are only vertical bars and so you seem to be more free
but with all that conditions on the whole are worse, they are
more inhuman. Whereas at San Giovanni you couldn't leave
your cell and walk about in the wing, in the Dozza you are free
to do so (always in the hours fixed by the regulations) so, there
are differences...But these are, you might say, pulsations within
the prison system. It's sufficient for something to go wrong
and the wider berth immediately restricts itself. If instead
of one prisoner hanging himself every 15 days there is one a
week, things immediately start to change. At the end of 1987,
precisely at the Dozza, there was a simple protest which the
prison authorities responded to with an armed attack against
the infirmary, led by the Nazi-style military commander of the
prison. In such situations prison changes in a flash.

But these pulsations inside particular prisons are related to
the pulsation of development and transformation in the prison
system as a whole, which is moving towards an opening. Why
is this? Because it corresponds to the development of the prison
system, the extension of its peripheral structures and the structures of the State as a whole. That is to say, there is more participation. This concept deserves to be looked at more closely.
Bear in mind, on the basis of what we were saying before about
contradictions, that the concept of participation is not at all

separate from the concept of separateness. I participate and in an initial phase of this participation I feel closer to the others who participate along with me. As this increases, however, the very process of participation isolates me and makes me different from the others, because each one follows his own road in this participation. Let's try to illustrate this concept better, because it is not very simple. You can see participation everywhere, in schools, in the factory, in the various functions of the unions, in school and factory councils, basically in the whole world of production. Participation comes about in different ways according to the situation. In the ghetto areas of cities, for example. Take the St. Cristoforo area in Catania [Sicily], for example. It is one of the biggest ghettoes in the town, with a high concentration of social problems, but things are changing, there are the family consultancies, whereas once the police couldn't even circulate there. How has this greater participation changed the area? Has it brought it closer to or taken it further away from the rest of Catania? That is the question. In my opinion, it has isolated it from the other areas even more, by making it even more specific. In my opinion, the aim of participation is to divide.

Prison is opening up to participation, there are structures for an inside-outside dialogue, such as "Prison-territory," let's say, composed of a bunch of swindlers, third-rate ideologues, representatives of town councils, unions, and schools, and delegations from the Bishopric. All this mob do is to get authorizations to go inside the prison based on article 17, and contact the prisoner, thereby establishing a contact between inside and outside. Any prisoner has one hundred, one thousand problems, he or she is like a patient. If you go into a hospital and talk to a patient, they have all the illnesses in the book. If you go into prison and talk to a prisoner you will find that he or she has a thousand problems. Above all, they are always innocent, didn't do anything wrong and their family is always needy. Well, the things prisoners always talk about. On the other hand, they each look after their own interests and, in any case, it's not appreciated in prison for someone to come out with, "Prison doesn't do anything to me, it's bullshit, rubbish..." no, that wouldn't go down well.

Participation causes further separation, a greater division inside the prison, because the few people of a consciously illegal disposition, that is to say the ones who really are "outlaws," stand out. In a prison population of, let's say, one hundred prisoners, you can already distinguish them in the yard. There you can see who the serious people are and who are not, and you can see that in many ways, from the many signals they give out. A whole discourse develops inside, based on the way they walk, the choices they make, the words they use. I know, many of these things can be taken the wrong way. I am not praising stereotypical behavior, what I'm saying is that there's a specificity inside prison. There is the prisoner who is aware of his job of being a prisoner, his qualification as a prisoner, and there is the prisoner who finds himself locked up by mistake, who might very well have been a bank manager, or simply a poor idiot. There is even the prisoner who finds a transitory systemization in prison, who sees prison as a passing accident (as short as possible) or a form of social assistance. I have seen people get themselves arrested just before Christmas because at Christmas they give Christmas dinner (you think that's nothing?), or to get properly cleaned up, or to be cured, because for many of them there is no other way to get treatment—and there is not one but hundreds of such cases.

But there is another prison population, those who pride themselves in being "outlaws," in being able to attack determined structures of the State their own way. This population is obviously not prepared to play the game of participation, so will stand out and be subjected to very strict isolation. That is why participatory prison is a prison of division, because it isolates. Not all are able to participate at the same level, not everybody accepts a dialogue with power. And the greater the participation, the greater the number of signals that come from it, the more the sectorialization of the prison world becomes visible.

Much remains to be said concerning the question of accepting a relationship with the prison institution. I am not going into all that today, having done it many times in the past. But let's take the question of parole. This is not something that can be summed up as a direct relationship between prison and

LOCKED UP

prisoner. Before parole is granted there is a whole procedure called "treatment" (the choice of the word is no coincidence, in that the prisoner is seen as a patient). The treatment is a series of decisions that he or she must make one after the other. It begins with a meeting with the psychiatrist, then there is taking a job inside the prison and that depends on your not having had any problems inside, so it's something that goes on for two or three years. That's it, you have to choose the road of bargaining with power well in advance. A legitimate choice, for goodness sake, but always in the optic of that desistence for which one says, "I don't feel like carrying on. I'm not damaging anyone and I'm going to take this road"...Well, if the guard behaves in a certain way I pretend to look at the wall that seems to have got very interesting all of a sudden; if there's a problem, I'm not saying a revolt, but a simple problem, I stay in the cell and don't go out into the yard. All this involves a choice, there is no clear alternative between detention and parole, that's pure theory, in practice it's not like that. Basically this problem exists for prisoners who have a coherence as revolutionaries. But prisoners in general, who find themselves inside for their own reasons and have never claimed any "political" identity no matter how rarified this concept has become, see things in terms of the practicability of a choice and do not pose themselves such problems even remotely. They have their own personal history and the way it fits in with what the law offers them. This itinerary takes two or three years, it's not something that happens in a day.

Of course, the prison of the future, which I believe will be far more open than the present one, will receive more attention so will be far more repressive and more closed, totally closed, towards the minority that does not accept bargaining, does not want to participate and refuses to even discuss anything. That is why I have spoken of the relationship between participation and division, a relationship that is anything but obvious at first sight. Things that seemed so far apart turn out to be close together: participation creates division.

So, what to do? We have often asked ourselves this question as far as prison is concerned. I've just read a little pamphlet. I hardly ever read anything about prison on principle, because it disgusts me to read these texts that go on and on about it. But, as I had been asked by some comrades, I accepted a "family" discussion, let's say. So, I was saying, I read this pamphlet. It was published by the comrades of Nautilus publications and contained an abolitionist text on prison, then an article by Riccardo d'Este. It was interesting, even though I didn't understand exactly what he wanted to say, I mean, whether he was making a critique of abolitionism or not, or whether he couldn't manage to do so completely, given that he was presenting this pamphlet. But there's something I don't like in this text and that is what I want to say, and when I see Riccardo I'll tell him. He condemned, absolutely and without appeal, those who have theorized or carried out attacks against prisons in the past. This judgement seems wrong to me. He says this...bear in mind that Riccardo is a very good comrade whom you perhaps got to know at one of his conferences here in Bologna...he says, "These attacks were nothing, they were senseless, in fact they have built the prisons anyway." But come on, dear man! You who are against efficientism in everything else, you say something that is eminently efficientist. What does "they built the prisons anyway" mean? Perhaps anything we do, when it doesn't produce the desired result, or doesn't reach the desired goal, isn't worth a damn? Sorry if I put this so simplistically, but the question of the attack on prisons is of particular interest to me. But no! Prisons must be attacked. That doesn't mean to say that once it has been decided to attack them they will all disappear. Or that because we have attacked them once we can say we are happy and will do nothing else to destroy them. I remember the attempt to destroy the prison of Sollicciano when it was being built. The attempt was made, but the prisons of Sollicciano were built all the same. But what does that mean, that the attack was pointless? I don't think so. Because if we were to come to the conclusion that Riccardo did, perhaps by a slip of the pen, as I'd like to think, we must condemn everything we do. Because nothing that revolutionary and anarchist comrades do is guaranteed to obtain the desired result and reach its goal in absolute. If that were the case we would really all be at peace.

Concerning Riccardo d'Este's text, it should be said that I don't just know his ideas from reading the pamphlet on prison, but also through having spoken to him. Riccardo is a fascinating person, but when you listen to him, or read him, you do well to separate what he writes from what he says, the wheat from the chaff, to see how much is valid and how much is the fascinating way he says it.

In my opinion, a separation of the kind he makes on the question of a possible interaction between reform and extremism doesn't exist. In reality there are not struggles that are reformist and others that are revolutionary. It is the way that you carry out a struggle that counts. As we said earlier, the way you behave with others counts a great deal: if I behave with my companion in a certain way, am I a reformist or a revolutionary? No, these are not the alternatives, it is more a question of seeing whether I am a bastard or not. And if I make a distinction between my way of being and my way of acting, my way of being in the intimacy of my relations with those close to me and my "political" way of appearing, then the distinction about reformism becomes valid. It is absurd to talk about these concepts in abstract.

The individual must make up his or her mind as to what their basic choices are in everything they do. If not, if they are continually copping out, they will clearly be revolutionaries in word alone, or they might conquer the world, but in order to do what? To enact a new theatre of Greek tragedy. The above distinction only exists in the world of the politician, that of the spectacle, representation (in Schopenhauer's sense of the term). If we reduce the world to this representation (don't let's forget that Schopenhauer lent his binoculars to a Prussian officer in order for him to take better aim and shoot the insurgents; this is the man who talks to us of the "world as representation," not the one that some anarchist readers have dreamed of from his book) then, yes, it is possible to make a distinction between reform and revolution, but again this is chatter. These abstract ideas don't exist in reality. There is the individual, with everything he or she relates to, and through this relating contributes to transforming reality, so you can't make precise distinctions about the things they do. All the theoretical distinction between reform and revolution is not as significant as was thought in the past.

...Now a few words on the question of efficientism.

This is a question that people work out for themselves. I come from a culture and a way of thinking that could be defined as efficientist, I was born in an efficientist atmosphere, I come from the school of efficientism. Then I convinced myself that this gets you nowhere. I convinced myself...theoretically, maybe in practice I am still the same, but at least in theory I can see the difference, that not all the actions one carries out necessarily obtain instant results. That is fundamental. It is important to understand this for many reasons, first of all because there is a tendency, especially among revolutionaries, to present the bill, and let's not forget that revolutionaries are greedy, they are exacting creditors...They are very quick to rig up the guillotine, they don't wait for anyone, this is something terrible. In fact, what is the guillotine of the revolutionary? It is the consequence of efficientism, because it reaches a certain point then begins to...I read something recently concerning the stupor caused by Lenin's writings. Many are shocked because Lenin ordered the peasant proprietors to be killed. That didn't surprise me at all. The killing of peasant proprietors is quite normal when done in the name of revolutionary efficientism. Either one is surprised at everything to do with efficientism, or one doesn't wonder at reading something of the sort because it is quite normal, a logical consequence of the choices made previously. If one wants to reach given objectives, there are certain costs, that is the concept of efficientism.

The question of efficientism concerns how to set out a struggle correctly, for example the struggle against the prison institutions that hang over each and every one of us to a certain extent. My grandfather used to say, "We all own a brick of the prison." "We have a brick each," he used to say. Not that he understood much about prison, but it was a well-known Sicilian proverb at the time. So, let's make prison become part of our whole intervention in reality, in intermediary struggles. The latter are the struggles that we carry out without expecting any great results because they will probably be recuperated, or because they are circumscribed. If these struggles are set out correctly, however, they always give some kind of result in a way that is different than efficientism. I mean, if social struggles are properly set out they reproduce themselves. And how can they be set out properly? First of all by getting away from the question of the delegate and the expectation of any outside support; in other words, by self-managing them. Then, they obviously shouldn't be carried out in accordance with the precise deadlines that are fixed in the laboratories of power, so they must start off from a different way of seeing things, from a logic of permanent conflictuality. These two concepts, self-management and permanent conflictuality, are then combined with a third: the absence of the need for immediate visibility. The effectiveness of a struggle does not come from a utopian vision of reality, but from the real possibility of setting it out in a way that eliminates any possibility of its being transformed into quantity and getting quantitative results.

This is possible. In fact, if we think about it, it is always possible. We often make the mistake of wanting to circumscribe the struggle in order to be better understood. By intervening in something specific such as the factory for example it is easy to see the characteristics: the struggle for wage increases, holding on to jobs, fighting pollution at work, and so many other things, and we don't see how prison can fit in to that, because we think that people wouldn't understand us as well if we were to widen the argument.

In itself the struggle, let's say in a factory, is always an intermediate one. How might such a struggle end up? At best one would reach the original objective, the workers would save their jobs, then everything would be recuperated. The struggle is recuperated, the bosses find an alternative to redundancy money, they find an alternative to dangerous work, they find further investment to improve conditions, etc. This kind of situation satisfies us, and in fact it is all right from a revolutionary point of view if the initial conditions of timing, permanent conflictuality, self-management of the struggle and everything else, were maintained throughout. But it is no longer satisfying if, in the name of efficiency, we prevent ourselves from including prison in it. Because for me the question of prison must be present in all the struggles we carry out like any other aspect of the revolutionary discourse. And if we think about it, it is possible to do something of the kind. When we don't, it is only in the name of efficiency, because we think that we won't be understood or that we might seem dangerous, so we prefer to avoid the question of prison.

A few words now on the abolitionist position. Bear in mind that I am not all that well prepared on the subject, first of all because I don't agree with the abolitionist position as I understand it, so I might leave something out. If what I say turns out to be lacking, well, correct me. I was saying, I don't agree with the abolitionist position, not because I want prisons, of course, but because I don't agree with a position that wants to abolish part of a whole that cannot be dissected. In other words, I don't think that it's possible to talk about abolition as opposed to attack. In other words, I don't think that it's possible to propose a platform to abolish one aspect of a context that is organically inseparable. I don't agree with proposals to abolish the judiciary, because for me such proposals don't make sense; or to abolish the police for that matter. That doesn't mean that I'm in favor of the judiciary or the police. In the same way, I don't agree with the abolition of the State, only its destruction. And not only do I agree to that but I am ready to act now towards such an end, whenever that is, even if it is extremely improbable in the short term. I mean, I am ready to do something, and can discuss what to do in terms of attack against this or that specific aspect of the State, and so also against prison.

In other words, as I see it the problem needs to be upturned. It is not a question of abolishing a part of the State, such as prison for example, but of destroying the State, obviously not completely and all at once, otherwise we would put it off to infinity. It would be like following that famous direction in history that is moving towards anarchy in any case, so we would end up doing nothing, waiting for this anarchy to come about by itself. On the contrary, I am prepared to do something today, right away, even against a part of the total institution, "the State," so also against prison, the police, the judiciary, or any other of the essential components of the State. This is the concept that I wanted to make clear.

What do these ideas actually correspond to? Let's spend another couple of minutes, don't get restless, I swear I won't bore you much longer. If you think about it carefully, the idea of the abolition of prison comes from a specific theoretical context, which frankly I don't know, but something I do know a bit more about was born alongside it. In America at the present time a number of universities are working on the question of the transformation of democracy within general philosophical ideas, but also in sociological theory. There are various American thinkers, the most famous of whom is [Robert] Nozick, who have examined the concept of a communitarian life without sanctions, without sentences, and without any instruments of repression. Why are they taking up this problem? Obviously because these enlightened people realize that the democratic structure as we know it cannot go on for long and they will have to find another solution. They need to look and see how communities could emerge without certain elements that are natural to the existence of the State such as prison, the police, State control, etc...This debate is not something marginal, it is at the center of political and philosophical ideas in American universities. And in my opinion abolitionism, correct me if I'm wrong, could be taken up by this movement. But this is a question that needs to be gone into by someone who knows more about it than me, I don't want to say any more on the subject.

Let's say that this kind of problem, especially for theorists like Nozick—there are also others but their names escape me at the moment—is an indication of some of the practical needs of the management of power. Evidently the historical model of democracy, for example [Alexis] de Tocqueville's book, is no longer acceptable. That is not the democracy we're talking about. Other structures are required today. Take a country like China. How will the future democracy of China be able to base itself on a model such as de Tocqueville's? How could a parliament with 26,000 members function, for example? Impossible. They must find another way. And they are working in that direction. We can also see a few signals here in Italy, in a different sense. Institutional transformations, as they say, that are the expression of the generalized malaise of democracy. But also intellectuals who seem far from democratic cover-ups such as [Michel] Foucault have given their contribution to the perfectionment of prison and a rationalization of the institutional structure.

Concerning Foucault, we could say that, at least as far as I know given that I know his work on the history of madness best, two basic lines of thought run through his work: one relates to overcoming and the other to maintaining a process in act. The result is that this theoretician always leaves something ill-defined. In all his proposals, even that concerning homosexuality, seen as both diversity and normality, it is never clear what he actually opts for. Ambivalence is characteristic of this thinker, and not only him but all those who are trying to keep themselves on an even keel. Basically, for him the prison question concerns an instrument whose use he is unsure about, he would like to do away with it but does not have anything else to suggest other than putting it in parenthesis. In fact, at a certain point, he gives the example of the *nave des folles*, which was a prison, asylum, orphanage, and rest home for old prostitutes, all at once. He writes that the *nave aux folles* was realized in a few days, that it takes very little time to realize it. At a time when society was expelling individuals who are *different* from certain cities (I'm not talking about homosexuals) it put them outside the walls. And these individuals, not knowing what to do, migrated from town to town, so at a given moment they were taken and put on a ship, the ship of mad people. This ship started to sail from port to port because nobody wanted it. A ship perpetually in movement. At that moment prison was created, as well as the asylum, the orphanage, and rest homes for old prostitutes, because at that time society could no longer tolerate their presence. Certain social functions had disappeared: that of the madman, who in medieval society was seen as one touched by God, and that of the beggar, who in Catholic countries was the object of charity, the basis of Catholic Christianity, don't forget. With the development of Protestantism, the beggar becomes an object of capture, so had to be held separate. When society can no longer use him, the figure of the beggar becomes superfluous. He disappears as the receiver of charity to become a prisoner. Today, this society no longer needs prison, the prisoner as a "thing" must disappear. How do you do that? By taking a ship and putting all the prisoners on it? But the prisoner as a "thing" does not disappear when the ship becomes a prison, in the way that the French did with those from the Paris Commune who were deported: they put them into pontoons, boats moored at Le Havre, and people stayed in them for 5 or 6 years, prisoners in a floating prison. Now society no longer needs prisons, as some enlightened social theorists are saying, so let's transfer the prisoners to another social institution. That would be the project seen from the abolitionist point of view. And here Foucault's discourse turns to perfection.

That's what I wanted to say. Now let's come back to the question of attack for a moment. I am always for the specific attack. The specific attack is important, not only for the results that it produces, not only for the effects it produces, that we can see before our eyes...None of us can claim to be functionalist, because if we were to fall into that contradiction we wouldn't do anything at all. So, first prisons need to be understood, because we can't do anything if we don't understand the reality we want to fight. Then they have to be made comprehensible to others. Then they need to be attacked. There's no other solution. They must be attacked as such. These attacks contain nothing of the great military operations that some imagine. I have always thought of these attacks as a day out in the country. One says to oneself, "I feel hemmed in today, in this anarchist space, (frankly I find them a bit depressing), and I want to go for a walk. Let's not stay shut up in this place, let's go out for a walk." By that, I don't mean a student-like attitude, because that's stupid, but let's just say without too much drama; it's always possible to go for a walk in the country, and it's not bad for your health...And without spending too much time discussing things and transforming a day in the country into a kind of crusade against all oppressors past, present, and future. No, something pleasurable, a day in the country is an activity that must also give us joy, but it is also something specific.

But prisons should also be attacked in the context of the struggle in general, that is, in the course of any struggle that we manage to undertake. And this is something that we have been saying for about ten years. No matter what we are doing, or what we are talking about, we must make prison a part of it, because prison is essential to any discourse. When we are talking about living areas, health, etc., we must find a way, and there is one, to include prison in what we are saying, denouncing all attempts to muffle it's potential to disturb social peace.

Bear in mind that prison is an element in movement, as we have seen, it is not something static and finite. For the enemy, prison is an element of disturbance. They are all always thinking about what they can do to solve the problem of prison. Now, their problem of prison must become our problem and we must think about it during the struggles we carry out, if we carry them out.

All this, of course, while awaiting the next insurrection. Because in the case of insurrection it will be enough to open up the prisons and destroy them for ever. Thank you.

THE STRUGGLE FOR
SELF-MANAGED SOCIAL SPACE

THE FUNCTION THAT SPACE HAS HAD THROUGHOUT THE DEVELopment of capitalism could be described as a real "history."

From the first "enclosures" of great masses of people into circumscribed spaces to the most advanced factories today, capitalism has tried to cut out portions of space to dedicate them to one specific use: the production of surplus value. Now, with the advent of the recent post-industrial development and advances in the technological process, the management of this space has changed profoundly. It has passed from a partial management to a total one. In this, Capital has had the support of power and the State. We think that it is important to reflect on the conditions of the relationship that exists today between social space and Capital.

No part of physical space is free from the interference of Capital. From celestial space to the ocean depths, from the mountains to the rivers, from the seas to the deserts, from the great metropole to the most out of the way villages. A series of relations between elements that seem far apart are linked by the common matrix of being objects of exploitation intersecting and covering each other. In this way, we can have the illusion that we are going somewhere far away, out of this world, as they say, then discover that even there, in that place, the mechanisms of Capital reach it and function perfectly. That explains why we are against environmentalism just as we are against any other "alternative" proposal that claims to do something against exploitation by cutting out one part of reality. Of course, we also start off from one part in our interventions, but we don't delude ourselves that we can really attack the enemy by staying within that "part." To move on to attack, we must go beyond fragmentation (single issues), a strategy that has been imposed upon us by Capital.

Now, of all the misappropriation that comes about through exploitation, the most serious, because it has the worst consequences, is that of time and of space. In substance the two are linked. Capital steals our time, obliging us to work and conditioning our life that becomes infested with clocks, obligations, and deadlines, right down to the tiniest detail. By stealing our time they prevent us from understanding ourselves, they estrange us from ourselves. They alienate us. Without time we do not even notice the theft of space any more. We need time to even notice the existence of space. To think, to listen, to dream, to desire. By living space in terms of distance, kilometers to be crossed, and moving from one place to another, we lose sight of our relationship with things, nature, and the world.

Capital has stolen our time from us (it needed it for production) and it has stolen our space (it needed it first as places of production, then as a system of control and repression, then to get general consensus). Now we are faced with the need to move toward expropriating our time and space. This expropriation will never be anything but violent and traumatic. Both for us and for our enemies. Our attack cannot fail to cause damage and ruin. It is in the logic of things, the logic of the class war. The project of power is global. It cannot allow "empty spaces" to exist. For the opposite reason, our project of liberation is also global. If we allow Capital to globalize power, we will definitely be dead.

Fortunately the road that power must cover is still a long one. We are only at the beginning of a design based on the division of reality into two parts, that are also physically separate.

After the global misappropriation of space (and time), Capital is separating it into two parts. It is no longer a question of the old fragmentation, but of a net division, a real wall between the included and the excluded. The first will be guaranteed a situation of privilege, power, high culture, projectuality and creativity; the second, a situation of survival, consensus, subculture, supine acceptation, lack of stimuli and perhaps even needs. In this perspective Capital and the State need the availability of the whole of social space. Nothing must escape their control.

Capital now disposes of technologies that allow it not simply the simple physical possession of space, but also its production. Think of the capacity of operating in "real time" communication between two points thousands of kilometers away from each other. That does not only change production (quality, variety, creativity, storage, etc), but also and principally the human arrangement of social relations (which are also economic).

So, Capital produces space on the basis of its project of exploitation and power. It transforms and destroys nature, modifies the cities and the countryside, destroys the seas, rivers, lakes, conditions stellar distances to its militaristic logic. Then, the spaces thus produced serve to channel individuals. That is how we end up in long lines of cars on the highway, in lines in the supermarkets. That way we find ourselves afflicted with chaotic trajectories, appointments we can't miss, fictitious interests that make us suffer and oblige us to make continual senseless deplacements. We move within the spaces that have been programmed for us that we only have the illusion of having "chosen." Our houses are full of useless, harmful objects. Space has become so restricted or, better, it has changed according to the needs of capitalist production, which must sell televisions, fridges, washing machines, bedroom furniture, and kitchens.

So, almost without realizing it, our time is disappearing into nothing and our space is being reduced to relating to objects that testify to Capital's persuasive powers. In this way we are conditioned to repetition. We make the same gestures, touch the same objects, push the same buttons. Repetition is, as everybody knows (but systematically forgets) the antechamber of consensus.

For its part, Capital must take away our space. It is practically obliged. And that is because it cannot leave room for our creativity, our capacity to do things ourselves, our desire for the new (which is then the stimulus first to find solutions that reveal undreamed of gifts of spontaneity and wealth). If Capital were to leave space to these forces of the individual it would not be able to maintain the pace of repetition that is indispensable to production, which, we must not forget, is only such on condition that it can also be re-production. Think of the efforts (aided by electronic techniques) that Capital is making to realize everybody's desires with the maximum diversification possible (but all centralized and codified). The great labels of fashion items, the fast-food chains, the advertising that exalts the taste of the individual within mass production, are no more than attempts to prevent other roads that could still be tried today.

Space is therefore produced and reproduced on the basis of consensus but also possesses considerable purely repressive aspects in the policing sense of the term. Control regulates various fluxes in the narrowest possible way. Raw materials and men, ideas and machines, money and desires. Everything is coordinated because everything has been preventatively homogenized; differences have become precisely that, they are no longer radically diverse. They have been reduced to the level of appearance and, in this new guise, exalted to the maximum, as the kingdom of freedom.

The strategy of power is therefore that of controlling "all" space in the same way as it controls "all" time. It is not just a question of police control but mainly control based on consensus and the acceptance of models of behavior and scales of values that belong to the technocrats of Capital.

What to do: Go in search of lost time? Of lost space?

Certainly not in the sense of a nostalgic trajectory in a backwards direction. In life nothing can turn back just as nothing ever presents itself the same way a second time around (nor in one that is absolutely different).

The old relationship with space left a trace. A sign of a physical place. The sign of people and their things. A road, a piazza, a country lane, a river, the sea and the sky, the woods and the mountains, had an open discourse with the individual who knew how to (and wanted to) listen to them. And affinity with other individuals took people to the same places, animated feelings, pushed them to action and reflection. There were individuals whereas now one hides like a part of a whole, of a crowd. Once we were exposed, often unprepared and vulnerable. Now we go under the cover of uniformity and repetition. We feel more secure because we belong to the flock. There are no points of reference in space, in time. Everything is about to be wiped out. Sounds, smells, thoughts, and dreams. Everything is being produced and reproduced. Everything is about to be reduced to merchandise.

In this perspective the struggle for social spaces becomes a struggle for the re-appropriation of the whole "territory" beyond and against the rules of control and consensus.

OCCUPATION AND DEFENSE OF SELF-MANAGED SPACES

By self-managed social space, we mean an urban space taken by a mass organization composed of individuals with the aim of using it directly, for their own aims (self-managing), with criteria that are beyond the logic of capitalist power and exploitation.

Compared to social spaces (school, barracks, factories, etc.) where an imposed function is directed at guaranteeing the interests of Capital, the struggle for the conquest of a self-managed social space constitutes an important and continuous attempt to practice freedom of action and expression that would be denied elsewhere.

This struggle is therefore, right from the start, constituted of a whole of anti-authoritarian actions that all start from a critical analysis of class society and its main functions. They are therefore struggles that adopt the method of self-management; they try to build freedom and social and individual equality, and so are indispensable for proceeding along the road of the abolition of power and capitalist exploitation.

The self-managed method is the only one that prevents the instrumentalization of the struggle by political parties, unions, council representatives, etc. But for that to happen, it is necessary that the method be employed correctly, guaranteeing freedom of decision in everything that is done during the course of the struggle.

This self-managing phase can be schematically distinguished in two phases: 1) self-management of the struggle for the conquest of social space through squatting; 2) self-management of the struggle for the defense of the social space through an opening towards the outside.

As far as the first phase is concerned, it should be said that the occupation can only be realized if it has managed to constitute a structure that we can define as a "mass" one, based on a specific affinity between the individuals that belong to it. Not so much an affinity of an ideological character, but substantial. The existence of common desires, common problems, make it possible, in a given moment, for a group of people to get together to struggle against common exploitation. It is a question of a point upon which it is necessary to be very clear. The class dominion of Capital is the cause of the present lack of self-managed social space and the contemporaneous presence of fictitious social spaces, precisely because within the latter, economic and social exploitation is maintained that serves the interests of the power of Capital. The struggle for the "real" conquest of social spaces therefore necessarily passes through the violent rupture with the dominant logic of Capital. The latter cannot maintain and will not maintain a passive attitude before our concrete initiatives of real liberation of social spaces, because these initiatives will constitute a considerable danger for it.

The State and Capital put specific limits on us, which, once they have been overcome, immediately put us in the condition of being "outlaws." To squat means to overcome these limits, it means to become an "outlaw." That is why it is necessary to make a violent break with the rules that have been imposed on us. That is why it is necessary to squat.

Coming to the second phase, it is more than obvious that we must know how to take our freedom ourselves, through our struggles. It is not written in any constitution that someone will give it to us. Also, with social space, no one wants to give it to us. Whoever has it, manages it according to their own interests (which are sometimes to not use them at all and simply leave them empty). In cases where these spaces are given to us, that depends on the fact that they want to control us, they want to ghettoize us. Instead of putting the classic cop on our tail, which costs money, so that they know where we are and what kind of things we are talking about. That is why, sometimes, they are quite happy to give us spaces, especially after we have begun our action of intervention in social reality. It is obvious that we don't need spaces of this kind, which cannot be called self-managed, because self-management is not just a question of managing the inside of the place.

We must therefore take our spaces ourselves, i.e. squat them. But it is not just a question of taking them, we must also defend them.

This defense must not only be a question of barricading ourselves behind a wall and putting barbed wire out front. We cannot simply limit ourselves to keeping the cops out. To defend the conquered social space it is necessary to grow, qualitatively and quantitatively, with outside intervention and the capacity to develop a discourse that has some meaning and doesn't simply reduce itself to the satisfaction of one's own interests or the exercise of one's own personal capacities. Music, poetry, etc., are all very interesting but, if they remain closed within the space, even squatted, it would just be another characteristic of the ghetto.

The best way to defend the conquered space is therefore the opening towards the outside.

To conclude we can say: the conquest of space only comes about with violent occupation, in that any other road (negotiation) cannot be covered. After, the self-management of space comes about with a defense that doesn't only consist of the minimal aspects that we could call "militaristic," but also, and mainly, in opening oneself up to the outside, in talking to people, meeting-up and linking one's own situation to the situation of the area one happens to be in.